NO MORE EXCUSES

Inspirational Poetry For Everyday Life

JAMES HUDSON, JR.

For additional copies of this book contact:

jhudson504@gmail.com

Printed in the United States of America
Wise Publications
~ *Custom Book Manufacturing* ~
809 East Napoleon Street
Sulphur, Louisiana 70663
337-527-8308
wisepublications@yahoo.com
www.wisepublications.biz

Acknowledgements

I would like to thank my parents, James Sr. and Rebecca Hudson. Without you I wouldn't be here and would've never found the motivation to publish this book. Daddy you stayed on me about doing something with a manuscript I'd been sitting on forever. I also want to thank my aunt and uncle Harold Sr. and Joann Lee. Paran you are the one who told me that my poetry was good and should be shared with the world. My cousin Boo who's been my lifelong big brother. My best friend Clifton James. My grandma, my uncle Harry, Nanny, aunty Pull, aunty Reetha. Chilita, Joe, Crystal, brother Kelly, Wop. You all contributed to my life and helped me somewhere along the way. I am, and will always be grateful.

Foreword

This book was preserved for a purpose. In the waters of Hurricane Katrina the only unpublished copy of this book sat in the murky, brackish, mold infested waters of Lake Pontchartrain for weeks in a house where the winds blew the roof off as the waters rushed in to the ceiling. When I went to the house to retrieve the manuscript I just knew the waters had swept it away or erased the ink from the pages. But miraculously when I opened the box the book lay packaged and, to my amazement, all the words were crisp and clear, despite the mold and water stains all around the borders of the pages. I have concluded that it was indeed God's divine power that preserved this book and it's message... for a purpose. And that purpose is to inspire, motivate and uplift those who read it. And I thank God that not even the waters of Katrina could drown this message of power and positivity that took over 9 years to compile. May these words bless, inspire, and motivate you in every way.

— James Hudson's Jr.

Table of Contents

Acknowledgements .... **iii**

Foreword by James Hudson, Jr. .... **iv**

Chapter I
The Sweet Sound of Inspiration

Press On and Be Strong 3
We Can Make It 7
Across the Threshold 8
Come Follow Me 9
Hold Back the Tears 10
When the Sun Climbs 12
You Can 13
Unleash Your Greatness 15
A Book By It's Cover 16
Untreasured Jewels 17
A Word of Advice 18
Elevation 19
One of Us 20
Make a Wish 21

Chapter II
Love is the Color of Beautiful

What Love Should Be 23
Love Doctor 25
Your Knight in Shining Armor 27
A Pleasant Surprise 28
The Greatest Gift of All 29
The Kiss of Bliss 30
In Your Eyes 31
Invincible Love 32
Heaven Sent 33
Tu Es Bonita 35
Better Than Beautiful 36
Let Me Love Your Imperfections 37
Yearning 39
So in Love 40
Our Love 41
No Comparison 42
My Wish Come True 43
Don't Wanna Be Lonely 44

Basking in Your Beauty 45
Two Years Worth of Lovin' 46
2 Sweet 47
A Special Secret 48
Anticipation 50
Be the One 51
By My Side 52
Do You Remember? 53
Enraptured 55
God's Gift to Men 56
He, She, and They 57
Is it Mutual? 58
It's Real 59
Let's Make it Last 60
Lover's Journey 61
Magic 62
Merger 64
Missing You 65
My Special Valentine 67
Only a Dream 68
Perfect Match 69
Something About Ya' 70
Taken Away 71
With You 72
Thankful 73
Thoughts of You 74
Unimaginable 75
Vacancy 76
Waiting for You 77
Waiting on Destiny 78
Walk With Me 79
What I've Been Missing 80
A *Real* Man 81

Chapter III
Enter His Gates (*With Praise*)

Lover of My Soul 84
I Believe 85
Son of a...King 86
I See You 87
Princely Presence 88
My Shining Light 89
Can You Believe? 90
It's Your Choice 91
Lay Me Down 92
Casually 93
Dream Home 94
Godly Prayer 95
He's All I Need 96
Homesick 97
Send 4 Me 98
Lost Without You 99

Chapter IV
The Way of the World

A Girl Named Katrina 102
No Justice 105
The Devil in Disguise 107
Signs of the Times 110
History's Miseries 112
Listen to the Silence 114
Inner Demons 115
Grave Loss 116
Unfit Critics 117
It's Time to Change 119
Praying for a Better Day 121
Just Thinking 122
*Sin*Sation 124
The Answerless Question 125
What Happened? 126
The 'Hood Ain't Good 128
Voice of the Ghetto 130
Redirection 133
When Angels Cry 135
A Call to Action 138
A Better Outcome in Mind 140
Blasphemy 141
Check Yourself 143
Get Serious 145
Time Will Tell 147
When Will it End? 149
Unjust Satisfaction 150
Unsatisfied 152
What Will it Take? 155
Time to Change 156

Chapter V
A Mile in My Shoes

My Life 159
Fallen Angel 160
Life Lessons 161
Made Me STRONGER 163
360 166
Ain't Enough 168
Ain't Going Back 170
Explicit Refusal 171
Through My Struggle 173
Close My Eyes 175
Ambition 176
Hidden Treasure 177
Just a Man 178
My Sole Aspiration 180
Non-Compliant 181

On My Own 182
Revolutionary 183
UNSTOPPABLE 185

Chapter VI
When Love Hurts

When Love Hurts 187
I Should've Known 188
Inadequate 189
Never Again 190
Could It Be? 191
Cold Turkey 192
Concrete Heart 193
Relief 194

Chapter VII
In The Belly of The Beast

Swirlin' 196
Dysfunctional Residence 197
Bird Song 199
Infected 200
Nightmare 201
A Prisoner's Dream 202
X-Ray Vision 203
Through the Storm 205
Resurrection 207

Chapter VIII
It Takes a Village

True Love (To Mama) 210
Definition of a Family 211
Birth of a Friendship 212
I Appreciate You 213
Maternal Devotion 214
Friendship 215
So, So Special 216
Mother 217
Words of a Friend 218
Your Seed (To Daddy) 219

Afterthought 220

About the Author 220

For God

Chapter 1

The Sweet Sound of Inspiration

Press On and Be Strong

Press on
In the midst of the storm
And press on
When everything's gone wrong
Listen, stay in the kitchen
Cause it won't last long

Press on
When you're down and depressed
Feeling trapped in a death grip of stress
And when your spouse and family get you upset
Just press on
And never let 'em see you sweat

Press on
When they stare at you and tease
Crack jokes and call you obese
Sometimes people can be so mean
But press on
For your beauty has yet been seen

So press on
Streetwalker with no home address
And press on
When it's cold and you need a place to rest
Though in this world you may have much less
Press on...for your treasure awaits in the next

Now press on
Young man confined to the wheelchair
And be strong
Cancer patient who's losing her hair
At times I know you might get scared
But press on
Because God cares

So press on
Alcohol and drug addicts
And be strong
When you're sick and got to have it
It might be tough but be consistent at it
And pray to God for the strength to kick that habit

It's tragic, but press on
Young kid doing that ten year bid
And be strong

Pregnant mom wondering who the dad is
And to the wife whose spouse is abusive
Be strong
Until you find cupid

You've got to press on
Even if you're deaf and blind
And be strong
Troubled soul thinking of suicide
And to the frightened child with a secret to hide
Darling be strong
And wipe the tears from your weary eyes

Press on
If you're stuck in the projects
With bad credit and broke pockets
And hard times got you signing flopped checks
Continue to press on
Until you find success

Press on
Little girl who grew up too fast
Baby be strong
Though every man has treated you bad
And in spite of all the pain in your past
Princess press on
For there is still joy to be had

So press on
Family members who've suffered a loss
A loved one's gone and you feel so distraught
Always carry them in your heart and your thoughts
And press on
Cause they're smiling at you wherever they are

I know it's hard, but press on
Lonely one with no mate
And be strong
When you're at home all alone with no date
Though inside your heart may desperately ache
Press on and patiently wait
And one day you'll find your soul mate

And I must say press on
To the prostitute on the avenue
To survive, what awful things you've had to do
But even if what they say about you is true
Still press on
For there's someone who will love you for you

So press on
Facially disfigured and maimed
And be strong
Despite the hurt and the shame
I urge you, press on and maintain
For you are special even though your appearance has changed

You've got to press on
Young angel with low self-esteem
You're different
And don't fit in with the rest of the teens
But even though you're not this year's prom queen
Press on
For you can achieve your dreams
So spread your wings

It won't be easy, but press on
Parents of children gunned down in the streets
And be strong
Though it seems you've loss your hopes and your dreams
And in spite of how hard it maybe
Press on
But cling tenderly to their memory

Like wise, press on
Struggling tenants recently evicted
And be strong
Mom and dad whose baby go convicted
And to the young girls in abortion clinics
Don't hate yourself
We've all made poor decisions

Press on
Shattered rape victims
And be strong
Battered wives whose husbands hit them
Precious lady get him out of your system
Cause if he's got to hit you
Then you don't need to be with him

Keep pressing on
Faithful workers recently downsized
Though the news comes as such a surprise
Now the bills are starting to pile
And the loan got denied
But still press on
Until you find a job to provide

And press on
When they say you ain't good enough

And be strong
When things are tough
And you're flat out of luck
You must press on
And pull yourself out of that rut

Press on
When you fail
And you hate your work detail
Hold on and persevere
Until you prevail

Press on
When life hurts
And you're being harassed at work

Press on
When your car's repossessed
And you flunked your college exam test
Just remember... life's not over yet

Press on
Soldiers at war over sees
With injuries both physically and mentally
You have served your country valiantly
Now press on
And return to your families

Press on
If you've suffered a miscarriage
And press on
When the fire has died in your marriage
And the affair has caused so much damage
Do your best to press on
And find a way to manage

Your friends might leave you when you need them
But press on
Sometimes your children rebel and you can't reach them
Still press on

Keep in mind it's an imperfect world
Into which we've been born
So when the going gets tough
We must press on

"No weapon formed against you shall prosper"
Isaiah 54:17

We Can Make It

We've all experienced joy
But often there's adversity
These are the times that we must keep our heads up
Strive to be all that we can be
Like the trees of old we must endure the winds
And destruction that follows the terrible storm
We must make a commitment to last,
Stand tall, and stay strong
Words can not explain
Some of the pain that some go through
The many tears that get held inside
With no one to cry them to
But the good thing about trouble
Is that it doesn't last always
The clouds may be gray and dreary right now
But one day they'll be replaced
By the sun's beautiful, peace-flowing rays
In a marathon it's never the fastest runner
That makes it to the finish line
But the wisest, the watchful
Never stumbling, because he takes his time
Likewise we also must take our time
And run the good race
And in the end, when we reach the finish line
There's nothing that could compare to the smiles
That will be on our faces
We can make it

ACROSS THE THRESHOLD

Cross the threshold
To the next sector
No turning back
It's time to bless the
Transition from the past
To present day
Don't be afraid
Your future awaits
And may it blaze
With triumphant possibilities
Your options are plentiful
Approach your destiny willingly
It is your fate to be great
Just be wise
And minimize your mistakes
Treat everyday
As if it's made just for you
And give your best
To whatever you do
Seek ever to improve
As you pursue your journey
Across the threshold, no turning
Until it's over
So march on soldier
A million dreams await...
For you to grab ahold of

Cast aside the shackles of fear and doubt
And pursue your dreams with reckless abandonment.
Because then, and only then, will you make your dreams come true

Come Follow Me

Let's expand
Leave the ghetto for the Promised Land
I'll be like Moses with the staff in my hand
To divide the tides
That against us do rise
Now's the time so
Come young and old
March in step with me
There's nothing that can hold us
If we press collectively
Lets us be as a sea
Rushing towards destiny
In essence we
Possess the keys
That'll make us free
From the mandates of Pharaoh
And nefarious arrows
Shot by the bows of injustice
In this corrupted republic
Now come follow me
And I will lead
Like a shepherd who guides his sheep
Where the grass is green
And it's safe to graze
I'll teach you the ways
To disengage
From the shackles that hold you in place
I'll show you the ways
To overthrow all the foes
That you face
Such as ignorance
Lack of confidence
And the poisonous toxicants
That addict and pinch our common sense
Now comc follow me
Pretend its '63, and I'm Dr. King
There's no stopping the
Force of a stampede
If we stand for a cause that we believe
We all have dreams
Now let's make them realities
For us to succeed is not a fantasy
Jump off the bandwagons please
It's time to change the mentalities
We've been programmed to embrace
We'll never be nothing is what they
Constantly say
But the message I convey
Is believe in self
Achieve your wealth
Receive your help
From the One who
We pray to
Then watch your life bloom
Like the flowers in June.
Now come follow me

To all who would listen,
The voice of wisdom resonates across the globe,
Pleading with the hearts of men

Hold Back the Tears

Hold back the tears
When nobody seems to care
And your world feels alone
So cold and unfair
Hold back the tears
In spite of how hard life has been to you
Refuse to bathe in self-pity
No matter what you went through
Decline to let the droplets fall
When the lies tear your hear apart
Stand tall in the face of it all
Because life is just too short
To be held captive
By despair and anguish
There's beauty in every moment
Despite how tough the pain gets
Actions are the language
By which our soul communicate
To be sad when drama invades
Often adds to the weight
Instead of breaking down
Put a smile on that beautiful face
And let the glow of positivity
Warm its way through your day
Hold back the tears
When you've been betrayed by someone you trusted
Staring at the walls
Feeling naive and disgusted
Hold back the tears
When shocking secrets have been revealed
And you're struggling to stay awake
From a nightmare that seems so real
I know it hurts
But put down those sleeping pills
Dig deep inside your soul
Use your inner-strength to heal
And hold back the tears

When the dams are about to break
Harness your energy and thoughts
On something good to concentrate
Hold back the tears
Though your life may be a wreck
Let not the rivers flow
From the wells of duress
Hold back the tears
When you're afraid and scared to death
Grab a hold of your emotions
And guide them to a place of rest
Hold back the tears
Like a cloudless Summer sky
Give not that which has hurt you
The pleasure of seeing you cry

Cast your cares on the Lord
And He will wipe your tears away

When the Sun Climbs

When the sun climbs
Our cares of yesterday
Will evaporate at a rapid rate
The golden rays
Will ease the pain away
When the sun climbs the stormy skies
The dark and dismal times
Shall run and hide
And every tear we've cried
Will be dried and nullified
When the sum climbs
Across the horizon on a pair of eagle's wings
To reign upon the throne like a regal king
The suffering of our worldly affairs
Will slip away into thin air
When the sun climbs
Like a yellow spider on a mission
We'll possess a deeper wisdom
And every bad decision
Will be forgiven
When the sun climbs
The walls of a new day
On the other side awaits
A cleaner slate
From which to regroup our lives
When the sun climbs...
It tells yesterday good-bye

Today should be a new and improved version of yesterday

You Can

Anything you choose to
You can pursue it
Like the tennis shoes
You can just do it
All it takes is some initiative
If you want to receive
You've got to give
The fact is it just takes some time
In life there are mountains to climb
But if you reach the top you'll find
A treasure that shines
What I'm trying to say is you can rise
Above discrimination, and lack of education
You can rise above the past
And what happened with mom and dad
And the money that went fast
You can make it the right way and make it last
Anything you think you can't...you can
The future's in your hands
You command the out come of your tomorrows
What you do today
Will pave the way for either joy or sorrow
For you can overcome racism, drug addiction
And the stigma of having been to prison
You can change your condition in time
Broaden the horizons of your mind
And if you try
You could neutralize your troubles
No matter how hard the fight
Don't give up when facing your struggles
Dust yourself off and stand tall after you stumble
'Cause you could make the world rumble
With the infinite strength you have inside
Apply your drive to self-enhancement
And there's no boundary to the advancement you could acquire

You could build empires
Like the Incas and the Mayans
And inspire the next generation
With the hunger and determination
To become a greater nation
And make the world a better place for
Our sons and daughters
Stop the trigger play in our headquarters
Cause we can be much more than gangbangers,
Dope slangers, and strangers to our seeds
We can be teachers and role models to our offspring
Always believe that you can achieve
Because anything you think you can't...you can
The future's in your hands
Bottom of the ninth
Either you strike or hit a grand slam
Either way, it's up to you where you stand
So always believe that you can...
Because you can

As the reflection of God Almighty,
You can do ... overcome ... and be ... anything!

Unleash Your Greatness

When I write
It's like my mind ignites
As thoughts take flight
Like bats using sonar sight
I ignite the pad when I glide with the pen
On every line knowledge written
When I'm scribbling or spitting
Just listen
'Cause what I'm kicking is uplifting
It's my mission
To be the voice that's missing
Among those who need to hear
The sound of wisdom in their ear
Spoken clear with no fear
The time is near
For us to appear
In the front instead of the rear
So put on your gear
And let's do what it takes
To escape
And elevate beyond first base
To a higher place that awaits
Where our fate is to forever be great
Why settle for second-rate
We deserve more than crumbs off the plate
Why isn't someone irate
At the fact that we're stuck in this state
It's time to embrace
A better way for our race
Let's erase the hate
Jail crowding and death rates
It's time to penetrate
Success no matter who hates
It's never too late
But it's on us to do what it takes
To demonstrate
To the world... That we can be GREAT!!

Don't sit around saying what should be done--make it happen
Don't sit around dreaming of what you can be--become that

A Book By Its Cover

You can not judge the essence of a thing
By what your vision beholds
Just because the outside doesn't glitter
Doesn't mean it's not gold
So many overlook fortunes
For failing to stop
And inspect a little closer
That dirty old rock
See what they didn't know
As I will tell
Is that the dingy old outside
Is only a shell
For if you dig deeper
Inside you may find
A wonderful treasure
that brightly shines

Man looks on the outward appearance,
But God judges the heart
-Samuel 16:7

Untreasured Jewels

A woman's body used to be
A thing of beauty
And sacred
But then comes pornography
Where she
Displays it
As if she hates it
Makes it
Seem so filthy
When it was meant to be
The epitome of intimacy
Gives me the creeps
And brings chills to my soul
For something so honorable
To be brought down so low
It's pitiful
Don't we know
That we're supposed
To treat
Our ladies respectfully
Certainly they are worthy
And deserve to be
Regarded properly
And in the right context
And with utter respect
For they are jewels
And they are precious

"This is now bone of my bone and flesh of my flesh...
She shall be called woman..."
--Adam (Genesis 2:23)

A WORD OF ADVICE

Rearrange your concepts and figurations
Reverse the blind steps
That kept you in tribulations
Delay the mind set of stress and manipulation
Then renovate your estate through innovation
Cause failure is caked with heartache and frustration
Decisions you make
Will castrate or elevate 'ya
The way to success
Is paved with patience and dedication
In order to progress
Stay away from hesitation
If you believe then there is no limitation
Your boundaries are as far away as the constellations
All it takes is faith and concentration
Time is too valuable to be wasted
So make sure your hard work is compensated
Give it your all and your wall can be decorated
Like all the other success cases that made it
When opportunity is offered—you'd better take it
And if anything gets in the way...then terminate it

"A wise man will hear and will increase learning
And a man of understanding will attain wise counsel"
-Proverbs 1:5 (King James Version)

ELEVATION

My concentration
Is constantly contemplating
On methods of elevation
Meditation increases acceleration
Of my pursuit to reach the roof
Ambition is in my roots
As potent as 90 proof
Through
Persistence and dedication
I'm reaching my destination
To succeed
'Cause I believe
It's possible to achieve
Whatever you can conceive
I feed on positive energy
Mental visions of all my dreams
Becoming reality
Like the eagle I spread my wings
And glide upon the breeze
Of opportunities
To open doors you need the keys
Success is gleaming within my eyes
Accomplishment requires drive
Therefore I
Steadily climb
As I...
Steadily rise

No patience, no elevation

One of Us

I don't hate you
Because you're still human too
Even if you have AIDS
I'm not afraid...
Because you're still human too
Though I
Despise the things that you do
And I
Dislike the flings you pursue
In my heart I will always have love for you
It's true...
Because you're still human too
Even though you have your ups and your downs
For real
And no one seems to want you around
I feel
That eventually you're 'gonna rebound...
Because you're still human too
I know
You came out the closet last week
For sure
And the whole world calls you a freak
But guess what?
They can judge you till their faces turn pink
And guess what?
It doesn't matter what anyone thinks..
Because you're still human too

"Let he that hath no sin cast the first stone."
(John 8:7)

Make A Wish

Close your eyes
Make a wish on this day you were born
For one moment
Forget the trials and thunderstorms
Make this moment your own
As you reminisce on yester year
How the Lord mighty and strong
Has given you blessings far and near
Open your eyes and witness
A special wish come true
For it's a joy to behold
The blossoming of your own fruit
Now make a wish, don't hesitate
Utter your heart's most tender plea
For the Shepherd is able to make
Your dreams a reality

"Ask, and you shall receive..."
--John 16:24 (New King James Version)

Chapter 2

Love is the Color of Beautiful

What Love Should Be

Matching shirts and shorts
Holding hands and taking walks in the park
Missing you and having thoughts when we're apart
Being real, straight from the heart
Baby that's what love should be
Taking you places I know will make you smile
Hitting the mall to get you all the fashion and styles
The ride break down, I'll walk a thousand miles
To make it worth your while
To make you proud
'Cause baby that's what love should be
Apologizing when I'm wrong
Late night conversations on the phone
Love letters, cards, and poems
And making love until the early morn
Baby that's what love should be
Tickling and cuddling
Kissing, hugging, and touching
No arguing or fussing
Taking our time, no need for rushing
Baby that's what love should be
Whispering softly under covers
And taking care of each other
You come home, I'll have your dinner on and bath water running
'Cause you're my wife and I'm your husband
The only one I give my loving
Baby that's what love should be

Love should be us
Should be trust
Making love, not sex or lust
When you're tired I'll be your crutch
Being there for you is a must
'Cause baby that's what love should be
Whether thick or thin
I'll be your lover and friend
From beginning to end
'Cause that's what love should be
Even when the money ain't right
And things are kind of tight
I'll be there right by your side
To wipe the tears from your eyes
And I ain't lying
'Cause baby that's what love should be
Love should be you and me for eternity
Living happily as a family
I want to bring you joy, not make you mad at me
Give you my all, not hold back of flee
When it's time to face responsibility
Are you feeling me?
'Cause I mean every word you see
In this poetry
I just want you to know that if you chose me...
I'd give you everything love is supposed to be

"The "perfect relationship" may or may not exist.
But if I can't reach perfection, I'd like the closest thing to it."

LOVE DOCTOR

I will heal your wounds
And take upon your hurt
I will feel your pain
And stand in your stead
And take the blows that were meant for you
I'll be your strength where you are weak
If I have to suffer, I will suffer for you
I will help you walk
If you grow weary
I will be the tree
You can pick sustaining fruit from
I will see for you
So you can close your eyes to rest
I will be your warmth
And soothing touch
You can talk to me
And I will listen with all of my senses
You can cry to me
And I will cry with you
If there is nowhere to lie
You can lie on me
When you need to be embraced
I will do so with tender arms
If you are feeling doubt
I will reassure you
Whatever happened in the past
Let my love ease the pain
Accept my adoration
Let me prove your insecurities unfounded
Allow me to bring out your beauty

And proudly reveal it to the world
I will be your source of nourishment
A flowing well for whenever you thirst
I will wait upon you like a servant
Like a mother would her dear child
I will heal your wounds
Because I don't want you to hurt
I will take upon your pain
Because I can handle it
I will be everything you need me to be
And help you emerge from your cocoon
To live as the dazzling butterfly
You've always been inside

*"When the body hurts it needs a physician
When the heart hurts it needs a love doctor"*

Your Knight in Shining Armor

Since my counterparts are causing you stress
Let me be the one who brings you happiness
With my heart let me adore you
From the start I'll never bore you
What they say about men is so true
Some do cause unnecessary pain
But let me be the umbrella to your rain
I'll massage the strain
And wipe away the stain
Of tears that trace your face
What you wanted from him let me replace
It's a disgrace
The way some treat their women
And if you ask me, I can't comprehend it
The way they make things hard on you
There's already so much that you go through
So what I'd like to do
Is help you get through your struggles
Be the man who carries you over the puddles
I'll cuddle
Next to you and soothe your soul
Let you know that you are beautiful
And cherish you 'cause you are wonderful
I'll hold you close
Just to let you know that I'm there
Treat you better than most
And do everything to show that I care
I'll pull up a chair
And listen
Bring me all of your problems and tension
And I'll do whatever
To make you feel better
Whatever it takes
To put a smile on your face
In every way
Make life for you a better place
Whatever would make you happy I'll do it twice
I'll be your knight
In the armor that shines so bright

"Chivalry and romance are the icing on the sweet cake of love."

A Pleasant Surprise

Let me hold you
And enfold you
With the length of my arms
Come here where its warm
I'll shelter you from the winds and the storms
So disarm your alarms
And relieve all the guards
That patrol the gates to your heart
Guarantee I'll be
A glare to your dark
Lonely nights
Spent in fright while alone
With all my might
Let me right
All that's wrong in your life
It's my delight
To taste of the ripe
Fruit that's in your garden
As I gazed at the stars in
The sky
Saw the answer to what I prayed in the sparkle in your eye
But when I cast out my line
Into the depths of the sea
Never expected to retrieve
One so perfect for me
Ironically
I didn't believe
That the bait on my string
Could lure anything
Of your pedigree
When you said unto me
That I was the chosen
My heart froze in
To shock
Like a yacht parked at dock
Or a clock that just stopped
Very few can look at a rock
And see the diamond inside
But to those who can lies...
A pleasant surprise

"Some of the most precious blessings are hidden in plain view."

THE GREATEST GIFT OF ALL

He could've given me riches
Lots of diamonds and gold
Could've given me crisp dollar bills
More than my arms could hold
Instead He gave me something better...
He gave me you

He could've made strong
And brave like the lion
Could've given me wings like the eagle
So that I could soar the horizon

He could've given me beauty
As delicate as the petals of a rose
Or made me as elegant
As the soft wind that blows
But He gave me something better...
He gave me you

He could've taught me things
That no one knows
Could've made me wiser than Solomon
Or the ancient Pharaohs
Instead He gave me what He knew I'd love the most...
HE GAVE ME YOU!

"Delight yourself also in the Lord,
And He shall give you the desires of your heart."
-Psalm 37:4 (NKJV Version)

The Kiss of Bliss

In your arms
Is where I belong
Pampered by your charm
Safe from harm
In your eyes I see the fire
Of a love that burns brighter and brighter
My desire
For you is at an ultimate high
Like the birds that climb
Altitudes in the sky
It's like a beautiful picture
Of the perfect sunset
Cause every time I'm with ya
It's something I can't forget
When we met
It's like a beam sliced through my heart like a knife
Everything dimmed and all I saw was you in my life
What a sight
To behold the joy of two lovers
It's unmatched by any of the world's other wonders
Count the number
Of times your heart beats in a day
When love's real
There's things you feel
That words cannot say
Or convey
Exactly what's inside
Since we met I haven't even thought the words"good bye"
Wonder why
Everything has changed like this
Can't explain what happened to me after that first kiss
Ain't it bliss?

Meeting someone nice is like
A breath of fresh air on a stuffy day

In Your Eyes

Your beauty is heaven sent
Though truly I'm guessing it
Can be misleading
When people keep feeding
On what they're seeing
Rather than perceiving what lies within
Like when what I'm riding in
Determines the kind of friends
That I attract
But the fact is that
There's more to a soul besides the surface
What glitters like gold sometimes is worthless
But not in your case, I'm sure
Not with a smile so seemingly pure
And a glow that seems to endure
What ever life has shot at ya
I'm just glad I got at ya
And for the record, I'm not after
Your physical form
I need a friend I can call when it's cold and I wish it was warm
I'm fishing for all
I've sought but couldn't find
In these times
Of games and lies
Yet I have hope...
'Cause I see hope in your eyes

"The eye is the window of the soul"

Invincible Love

We will
Overcome
Every trial
That we face
We will
Leap above the hurdles
Of life
With strength
And grace
There may be times
When we stumble
But we will not
Fail
Against all manner
Of adversity
In the name
Of love
We will prevail
And though
There will be storms
The light of our
Joy
Will endure
Beaming brightly
Through the darkness
So strong and so pure

"Real love is relentless."

Heaven Sent

She's God's greatest gift to man
Other than life itself
And should be adored as such
Her worth and purpose
Should never be misunderstood
She's not a possession
For she's her own being
And she's not a servant
Here to meet man's demands
She's not a toy
Or something to be used or played with
Far from shallow or simple
She is complex and mystical
Her ways take time to understand
For she is a sharp thinker
Who's very crafty
She is the fertile ground
And giver of life
Like a beautiful garden
That blooms in the Spring
She is so wonderfully precious
And sweet
And lovely
And exquisite
Everything about her
Is to be appreciated
And thankful for
Her radiant beauty
And affectionate manner
The graceful way
That she walks
Her femininity
And sexiness
The taste and smell
Of her body

And the wonderful
Pleasure that it gives
Her voice
That is soft
Soothing
And seductive
She's fun
And full of love
So kind
And gentle
And special
She's the filler of all the voids
In man's life
She completes him
And makes him happy
She's his better half
His partner in life
His darling
And friend
Who's undeniably
HEAVEN SENT

"He that finds a wife finds a good thing
And obtains favor from the Lord."
(Proverbs 18:22)

Tu Es Bonita

Mami you're beautiful
From your pretty head to your cuticles
Your skin is milky smooth and you
Have captured my mental facilities
Anticipation of being near you is killing me...
Softly
To you I'm offering my heart's key
Open the door and enter
Become my center
Be my warmth during the coldest winters
From January to December
I want to be the man you remember

"Beauty is a hand that grabs your attention."

Better Than Beautiful

She's better than beautiful
Was my assessment of our first encounter
I walked away from the counter
Thanking God that I'd found her
In a rush
A million thoughts flushed
Through my mind
Deep inside
I knew you were the dime that I've been waiting to find
The kind that I could chill and be real with this time
And I can't lie
You're everything my life has been missin'
Small waste, a baby face, and a sweet disposition
Now I'm wishin'
That I could have a place in your life
For that right
I'd climb to the highest of heights
Lonely nights
Are all I've had lately
No one to cherish or to call my baby
All I'm saying
Is that I'm so grateful
You're the type with whom I could settle down and be faithful
Creatively find ways to
Give you my love and praise you
What I'm trying to say, boo
Is that you're graceful
From your pretty hair to your cuticles
And baby girl its true that you...
Are better than beautiful

"Beauty has a way of captivating its beholders."

Let Me Love Your Imperfections

Let me love the things about you
That you rarely show to others
Because my love is so strong
That I eagerly accept all of you
The wonderful and not so wonderful
Clearly you are beautiful
And breathtakingly attractive
But I want to get to know you so well
And be so trusted by you
That you feel
Comfortable enough with me
To share
The most personal things about yourself
I want to know those things
Because I want to love them
Because they're you
I'd like to know the real you
Not the outward shell
That's made to look a certain way
I want to know the you
That gets embarrassed or angry
And has real feelings
And emotions
I want to know the little things about you
That even you don't pay much attention to
I want to know the side of you that comes naturally
The way you act
And the things you do
When no one's around
I'd like to know
What you look like in the morning
When you're just waking up
I'd like to watch you brush your teeth
Or put on your clothes

I'd like to watch
While you shop
Or swim
Or do your job at the office
I'd like to watch
As you eat
Or read
Or talk on the phone
And I'd like to watch you
Sleeping softly
Looking cute as an angel
There's nothing I wouldn't accept about you
Nothing I'd dislike
So open up
And let me become intimate with you
Inside and out
Let me love everything that makes you who you are
Even the imperfections

If someone really cares about you,
They'll be there when the makeup's off,
And the hair's undone; whether you're sweet,
Or in a bad mood. That's when you know
It's real

YEARNING

Your beauty surpasses the visual
Options of my physical
Optical stimulation
The windows of my soul behold your celebration
My world without you equals devastation
You are the subject on which I'm meditating
Daily, hourly, secondly
Your presence is heavenly
To share a spot in your life is like
The splendor of the stars at night
I shine when I'm near you
I cry when I peer through
The atmosphere of your being
You're the reason I'm believing
In me
I'd choose you over eternity
Desire is burning me
Like fire internally...
Because with you is where I yearn to be

Desire is like a fire trapped in my soul

So In Love

There's a sparkle in my eye
At the thought of you
And a spell takes me over
That no one can undo
There's a glow inside my heart
That you put there
A feeling so wonderful
It has to be shared
There's a smile on my face
No longer a frown
A reason to look to the stars
And not toward the ground
There are tears in my eyes
But not those of pain
And my heart feels free
To try love again
There's hope and there's happiness
Come back from the dead
The prospect of a bright future
Lies just ahead
There are feelings almost forgotten
Back in effect
Which had gone into hiding
But are now ready and set
How great and marvelous
This change in my life
The clouds have disappeared
And now I see the light
And all is beautiful
Everything under the sun
I've fallen in love
Oh look what you've done

"Love is a natural, hypnotic high."

OUR LOVE

BABY U R MY TREASURE
I WAITED 4 U 4 WHAT SEEMS LIKE 4EVA
U FULFILL MY DREAMS AND GIVE MY HEART PLEASURE
BEYOND ECSTASY'S HORIZON
YOU ARE THE CLOUDS WITHIN THE SKIES IN
MY SOUL
U BRING WARMTH TO MY COLD
LONELY DAYS OF OLD
U STOLE MY HEART
NO, U EARNED THE MOST PRECIOUS PART
THAT I HAVE TO OFFER
I'M HARD AND ROUGH, BUT U MADE ME SOFTER
THE COST OF LOVE IS PATIENCE AND UNDERSTANDING
TO BE GENTLE AND NOT DEMANDING
AND WE'VE TRAVELED OUR JOURNEY
WITH BUMPS IN THE ROAD AND TWISTING AND TURNING
BUT THE FIRE'S STILL BURNING
NO MATTER HOW THE WINDS
TRIED TO BLOW IT OUT AGAIN AND AGAIN
BECAUSE WE'RE TRULY FRIENDS
TRULY LOVERS
TRULY SISTER AND BROTHER
AND I LOVE YOU LIKE I'VE ABSOLUTELY LOVED NO OTHER
I WANNA SMOTHER YOU WITH AFFECTION
COVER YOU WITH MY MANLY PROTECTION
BY LIVING LIKE I'M YOUR HUSBAND
NOT HESITATING TO MAKE THE NECESSARY ADJUSTMENTS
'CAUSE YOU'RE MY QUEEN
AND I'M PROUD TO BE YOUR KING
OUR WALK HAS SEEN THE UPS AND DOWNS
WE HAVE SMILED AND WE HAVE FROWNED
BUT WE'RE STILL AROUND
TOGETHER FOREVER...WITH GOD'S LOVE HOLDING US DOWN

Like a fortress...
Real love stands the tests of time

No Comparison

In my view
Everything else pales when compared to you
You're the sun, the stars, and the moon
A beautiful flower in full bloom
With a smile that shines like a pretty day in June
For you there's nothing I wouldn't do
Sacrifice my life if you needed me to
From first sight I just knew
There was no one else for me but you
Gone are my days of feeling blue
Cause you make my life brand new
And in my eyes
You're a precious butterfly
You're the clouds within my sky
And the wings that make my heart fly
The quench to my thirst when my lips are dry
I prayed for a wife
And you were the reply
You're the one who provides
All that I've ever desired
Your presence lifts my spirits higher
And just the thought of you ignites my soul on fire
And I'm no lier
You inspire me to build an empire
With you as the queen
I mean I'll construct for you
Your every dream come true
Cause in my view...
Everything else just pales when compared to you

"Every soul is a unique and precious work of art;
So consider yourself a divine masterpiece!"

My Wish Come True

Saw a miracle
When I opened my eyes
It's spiritual
When faith is applied
Never know what awaits
Maybe a surprise
As heavenly gates swing wide
Once we make up our minds
Dreams realize
And you know deep inside
When your blessing arrives
Saw two stars in the sky
Shining bright in my sight
And it felt so right
Gazing at the twilight
I made a wish
Staring in the sky that night
That you and I just might
Become like
Two stars holding hands in flight

Don't Wanna Be Lonely

I don't wanna be lonely
I guess none of us does
Because deep inside
We all wanna be loved

It's been so long
Since I've had someone to call my own
Someone I could cherish with my all
And hold in my arms

Many nights I mourned
With the pillow to hide my tears
Wishing with all my heart
That you were here

To ease the pain that I felt
When I was alone all by my self

That's why I took a chance
And opened up to you
I revealed how I feel
And that's something I don't normally do

So if it does happen
Like I hope and pray
I'm gonna give you the best I have
Until my dying day
I don't ever want to be lonely
Again I say
So I welcome you ...
Into my world to stay

"Loneliness is a vast ocean of emptiness;
But companionship is a feast of joy!"

Basking in Your Beauty

Your smile is lovely
And wonderful to behold
What a warm feeling
It sends through my soul
I'm glad that you chose
To open the doors
Of your world and invite me in
I'm excited at the prospect of having a friend
With angel eyes like yours
So sparkly brown...they glow
And show
A heart with beautiful things inside
I'm curious to find
The joy that being apart of your world could provide
And so I've
Decided that I wouldn't mind
Taking a moment in time
To bask in the presence of your heavenly shine

"Positive people radiate a wonderful energy that warms the soul."

Two Years Worth of Lovin'

Almost 2 365s
And you've been the apple of my eyes
All that time
I'm flying on cloud 39
I've found in you a sunshine so divine
I rhyme for you
I grind for you
And you have no idea of what I'm trying to do
To surprise you beyond expectation
To express love with demonstration
And dedication
I'm placing my heart inside your palm
Trusting that you will do it no harm
'Cause in my life you're the calm
To all of my storms
The subject of all my love poems
And the loving arms that keep me warm
In two years
We've endured the tears and the fears
The haters and the cheers
Unemployment and careers
'Cause love surpasses circumstances
It endures the acids
And corrosive tactics
That come against your commitment
Real love is relentless
For two years we've persisted
And existed
In spite of the elements around us
Katrina couldn't drown us
The critics frowned on us
But God's love surrounds us
And I savor His favor
Because our love is even greater
Even though it's two years later

2 years, 24 months, 104 weeks, 730 days, 17,520 hours, 1,051,200 minutes, 63,072,000 seconds = a whole lot of loving!

2 Sweet

Girl you're too sweet
You got my knees weak
As I crave for a piece
Of lovin' from a woman
Who's hotter than an oven
With a stack so fat
Give a brotha an asthma attack
Addictive like crack
But that's a fact
And not a flatter Boo
And I ain't trying to hide the fact that I'm after you
With my heart I wanna reach ya
And oh how I love your features
Been diggin' you ever since I seen ya
Cause baby you're a dime piece
So unique
And so sweet

"Like droplets of honey, so is the sweetness
Of a lover to the lips of a soul."

A SPECIAL SECRET

There's a special secret
I've held close to my heart
It gives me joy
And has me glowing like a shining star
It's a wonderful secret
I've never told anyone
Yet burns within my soul
Like the rays of the sun
My secret makes me smile
And tingle inside
It makes my days seem brighter
Like I'm on cloud nine
All the time
Because my life
Now has new meaning
And I'm beginning to have hope
That there may be reality
To all I've been dreaming
Throughout the years
You've been a treasure to me
And in ways you may not understand
You've made my life complete
The unfailing care
And compassion you've shown
Gave me strength to make it
Though the journey was long
And you stayed by my side
So I was never alone
I can't explain
How much that's meant
And I don't know the words to fully express

What a privilege it's been
To have you for a friend
But it makes me realize
That I want more
From the queen
Who's all I've ever hoped for
And more
I have developed feelings
That are solely for you
They've grown stronger in time
And now stand tried and true
This is the special secret
I've been clinging to
My secret is...
That I love you

"Some secrets are hard to keep."

ANTICIPATION

I await the day
When we'll know each other better
When there's no distance between us
And we can spend time together
And I await the day
That I could enjoy your smile
And just bathe in the warmth
Of your laughter for a while
How I await the moment
That I could share with you my heart
And trust you completely
With my most vulnerable part
I even look for the time
When I'll know the things you think
As if our minds were connected
Together on the same wavelength
But until those things are so
I will always fathom
And envision with hope
All of the wonderful things to come

"A blessing is the more wonderful
After having bathed in the warm waters of patience and expectation."

Be The One

Be the one
Who's there for me
The one
That brings clarity
Into my emptiness
And gloominess
Toppling the stress
Placed on a man
In a lonely world
Where he's a boy
Without a girl
Be the one
I feel in my heart
Whose touch I yearn
When we're apart
Be the one I need
Give me strength
And bear my seed
Build with me
Our dreams come true
Do with me
The things that lovers do
Let me be you
And you be me
Let us be one
In each other complete

With that special person in your life
The journey of a thousand miles
Seems like only a few steps

By My Side

I need you by my side
Because you're everything to me
By the joining of our souls
I'm more than I used to be
I need you by my side
With you I can stand tall
And no manner of adversity
Would be enough to make me fall
What an indescribable honor it would be
To have you next to me
My heart would weep with joy
From such wonderful unity
With you there with me
I can make it through the trials of life
Your steadfast love and devotion
Give me strength and encouragement to win the fight
So greatly I love you
In you my all will reside
And all I ask of you
Is to be there by my side

"Two are better than one..."
-Ecclesiastes 4:9 (NKJV Version)

Do You Remember?

Do you remember
The day that we met
How we could almost detect
An invisible bond connect
I still remember
How it was that day
I'll never forget how pretty
Was the smile on your face
You hesitated in the beginning
'Cause your heart had been hurt
And you had your doubts
That anything between us would work
That's when I had to pray
To the One Who would hear
I asked Him to please whisper
Comforting words in your ear
Bring her near
So I could fill her life with cheer
And remove the fear another created
Let me reverse the hurt that she's taken
He must've heard
'Cause you opened a crack for me
Cautiously let me into your galaxy
A world that captured me
Do you remember those days
Of writing heart-felt letters
As we sought
To know each other better
Do you remember
Those wonderful conversations
And how to hear each other's voice
Was something we couldn't wait for
Do you remember the magic
You felt inside
That sometimes made you cry
Do you remember feeling satisfied
And inwardly whole

From compatible communion
That filled your soul
And people said that you glowed
Do you remember being strengthened
When you were weak
Or had your mood uplifted
When your days weren't sweet
Do you remember what a blessing it's been
To have someone you could share your secrets with
And not be worried 'cause you knew they'd never tell even a hint
Do you remember
Having someone you could do the craziest things around
The kind of things
That would make others think you a clown
Do you remember
Having someone you could laugh with, and be yourself
Someone who understands you
Like nobody else
Do you remember
Being aroused beyond the physical
By one with spiritual and mental credentials
Do you remember
Looking up to that person
And how you felt
That they were someone you could learn from
Do you remember thinking...
God, this feels right
And it must've been a miracle
That brought this light into my life
Do you remember
The way he made you laugh
And how he did his best
To help you get over your past
Do you remember what we had

In the tough times
It's remembering the good that keeps you going.

Good memories are like sentimental albums
You can pull out and cherish and reminisce with.

Enraptured

Feeling trapped
Held captive by forces of love
Shattered dreams of self control
Flew the coup like a dove
So caught up
Emotions at maximum peak
Nervous and confused
Knees wobbly and weak
So enraptured
By this new part of life
Shedding thoughts of being a playa'
Excited at those of gaining a wife
So serious about commitment
A drastic change
From this to that
Slowly losing the grasp
On what was once in tact
The days
Once viewed as ordinary
Now bring
So much joy it almost seems scary
Pondering these things
I've concluded its source is above
Because no matter
What angle I look at it from
I remain enraptured by your love

Like leaves carried on a soft breeze
The joy of love lifts the heart into the clouds

God's Gift to Men

You are my treasure
Everything about you is a gift to me
Your smile and laugh
Your cheerful manner
And lady-like charm
Your concern
About the things that concern me
People don't look for gifts
To be inside of other people
But God's gifts are different
Than the gifts we give to each other
They aren't materialistic
He gives us not only the things we want
But also need the most
And sometimes His gifts
Come in the form of a living, breathing person
Someone He has shaped into the perfect person
For the one whom He will present them as a gift to
I know
For I am the recipient of a gift from God
That is so perfectly tailor-made for me
That it's mind blowing
And so joy- inspiring
My God has blessed me
With a very rare and precious fortune
All within you

Who can find a virtuous woman
For her price is far above rubies
(Proverbs 31:10)

He, She, and They

He...

God made man
And He was pleased
But Adam was alone
Without Eve
Without a woman
He's incomplete
For she's the garden
That bears his seed
And his helper
To achieve his dreams

She...

She's the Lord's
Most precious creation
And her beauty
Has no limitation
But there's a void
She feels inside
Without a husband
By her side
When she's with him
She feels alive
As his partner
And his bride

They...

It's magic
When two hearts meet
Becoming one and complete
He's there to protect and provide
She puts the sparkle in his eyes
Like the sun their love will shine
Until the end of time

God, in His infinite wisdom, created two beings with voids that only each other could fill

IS IT MUTUAL?

Many nights
I lie awake
Unable to sleep
Thinking of you
And wondering
If you're thinking of me
And I wonder
If all the hurt I feel
Is felt by you
If being separated like this
Affects you too
It drives me crazy
Can't even hear your voice
Wanting to be near you
But not having a choice
And I wonder
If you feel the same
If it would mean as much to you
To hear me call your name
And I wonder
If you ever feel under the weather
Because you've been waiting so long
And still haven't received a letter
And I wonder is there ever a time
When you wish you could feel my touch
As you lie comfortably
In the warmth of my clutch
Since we've been together
I've begun to feel these things
And I was just curious to know
If you ever feel the same

"The traffic of love flows so much better
On a two-way street."

It's Real

I know you're trippin'
Because of the moves that I make
But make no mistake
What I'm feeling
Is real and not fake
So Babe
That's the reason why
I'm showing you my
Sincere and genuine side
My playa' stats
I pushed that aside
'Cause that day I looked in your eyes
I saw something that took me by surprise
It blew my mind, I can't lie
Baby this is real
Gives me chills
Just thinking about how it feels
When I'm in your presence
Got me counting my blessings
That God gave me
I was so alone going crazy
But then you came and saved me
And gave me hope
Now I'm ready to go
To any limit to show
You that I'm serious
My love isn't mysterious
'Cause girl I'm really feeling it...period

"In today's world, the quality of being real is like the mythical unicorn... So rare and precious."

Let's Make It Last

True love
Given as a gift from above
That's what it was
That brought and bonded
Two hearts together
In joy we responded
But ran away when the stormy weather came
I can't blame you, because the pain hurts
So much against us
Yet we've 'gotta find a way to make it work
That's a must
Can't brush it away
Too much is at stake
In life if you want something
There's a price you have to pay
And the treasure
That we're hoping to purchase
Is the undying pleasure
Of sharing a life that's worth it
But if we really want it we're 'gonna have to work for it
Like the farmers working hard in order to reap a harvest
You know you reap what you sow
Have to water the plant if you want it to grow
You and I both know that we are meant to be
There's no way to deny that this is destiny
Can't see
Why we won't work for what's ours
Aggressively
To build a love that's solid as a tower
Baby let's get it together
Be strong in the face of whatever
And make this love last forever

"If it's worth having...
Then it's worth the effort."

Lover's Journey

Let's hold hands and walk on a journey
Together through a life filled with loving and learning
Together we could make our every dream come true
Its us against the world, just me and you
We could help each other when times get hard
And we could laugh together when we've been blessed by God
I feel in my heart that we could be happy together
It isn't perfect right now, but I promise it'll get better
You stole my heart by being so kind and sweet
I couldn't sleep thinking of how it would be with you and me
Now I'm hoping you're willing to pay the price
To be the woman and the queen of my life
If we could be together it would be so nice
I'd give you my all and make you my wife

Magic

Pulled up with your girls
But you stayed behind
Just one glimpse of your face
And I made up my mind
That you would be mine
I had to step in spite that I'm shy
'Cause what I saw in your eyes
Was a magical light that shines
And I couldn't lie
Didn't even try
Poured out my soul till it was dry
Inside I could've cried
The way it felt standing by your side
Made me feel like I was high on cloud nine
In just one moment in time
You stole my heart forever
Now all I think about is you and I together
Writing letters
Telling moms and thanking God that I met her
Ain't ashamed to sweat her
'Cause she's better
Than all the others put together
So whether I get you now
Or at another date
Somehow some way
'Gotta have her 'cause she's my soul mate
Girl you've got a shape
That won't quit
And a pretty face
I've got to kiss
If I had a wish
It would be you and me
L.O.V. and don't forget the E

You keep impressing me
With your fly steelo
That other guy's a zero
I'll be your hero
Scoop you up and take you where you're supposed to be
Buy you a crib, lay you on golden sheets
I know you're a queen
That's why I dream
And fantasize
That you and I
Will unify
Committed until we die
I'll hold your hand when you cry
Lay on my shoulder when you're tired
And let me be there for you
Care for you
And I'm prepared to do
Whatever it takes
To have a special place
And possibly set a wedding date
So we can share the rest of our days

"The birth of love is a miracle worth celebrating."

MERGER

Togetherness
What bliss
Two separate hearts
But as one
We exist
Sharing one body
One mind and soul
Exploration
Revelation
Watching love unfold
Climbing high
Reaching heights far and beyond
Molecular emersion
The perfect bond
Two images
With differences
Become an entity
Consequently
Fulfilling destiny

"When two become one...
The world has fulfilled its purpose."

Missing You

We used to be so close
You'd never see one without the other
And as my heart takes inventory
It's missing you that I discover
Tears stain my face
As I take that lonely walk down memory lane
Remembering occasions that brought us so much love
But now the love is lost
And I can't stand the pain
We used to make love
Like two angels descending from above
Whispering soft things in each other's ears
There was no limit to our love
Yes, we had our lover's quarrels
But they never lasted long
Before you knew it we'd be kissing and making up
And building our love so strong
So for now there is no happiness
At last our love is through
And from the time the rooster crows
Till the fat lady sings
I'll be forever missing you

"You don't miss what you had, until it's gone."

My Special Valentine

Tears stain my eyes
As I think of the love you bring
The way you pour happiness into my soul
The way you make my heart sing
That's why you'll always be my special person
Sweeter than the sweetest wine
So tasty to my lips
Will you please be my valentine
Like the rose in the garden
You're the apple of my eye
Better than Momma's red beans and rice
Tastier than grandma's pumpkin pie
I love you more than I can explain
More than a pretty day's sunshine
I'll be with you forever
But today would you be my valentine
Your love lifts me up high
Higher than the mountains and the stars
Having you is a special gift
Better than a parking lot full of brand new cars
That's why I will always cherish you
Forever until I'm old
And I'd rather have you, my love
Than a vault full of gold
For now we are apart
But we'll be together, it's just a matter of time
And although I won't be there to hold you
In my heart you're my special valentine

"Love is so awesome...
It has its own holiday!"

Only a Dream

I had a dream
That we were together the other day
In the park holding hands watching the kids play
We talked, we laughed
Even shed a few tears
We shared our hopes and secrets
And even our fears
You told me things
That lit up my soul
And as we connected
I felt so alive and inwardly whole
On that beautiful summer afternoon
Sitting side by side
On the bench breathing the cool
Fragrant breeze
Perfumed by the lovely flowers in bloom
That special day in June
Was one of the prettiest I've ever seen
Felt like Heaven to be in your presence
But it was only a dream

"What the mind hasn't achieved in the real-world,
It will endeavor to do so in the realm of dreams."

Perfect Match

We fit together
Like pieces of a puzzle
And we've found in each other
What no one else had to offer
I was lost but now I'm found
And my heart's back on solid ground
As love abounds
Where once was heartache and pain
All my wounds washed away the day you came
Now your name is etched upon my soul
And having you in my life has taken a toll
On every single part of me
I'm gonna be
Loving you for eternity
It's burning me deep inside
With emotion so potent it lifts me high
That's why
I dedicate to you my life
So don't be surprised
If you see tears in my eyes
When I drop to one knee
Coming out with the ring
As my voice sings
Please be my Queen
I'll be your King
The one who'll give you everything
Your heart desires
Was once a "playa" but now I'm retired
It's like something from heaven just made us attract
And I know in my heart...
That you're my perfect match

"Some people are just meant to be together."

SOMETHING ABOUT YA

There's something about you
That makes me smile when you come to mind
There's just something about you girl
That hits the right spot at the right time
There's something about you
That gives me goose bumps when I hear your voice
Makes me want to take you shopping
For the clothing of your choice
There's something about you
That makes me feel so warm inside
Think of me as a brand new car
Hop in and take a joy ride
It's hard to believe that you're so sweet
Like strawberries and whipped cream
And there's just something about you'
That makes me wanna put you on my team
There's just something about ya

The angels in heaven smile when two hearts attract

TAKEN AWAY

Loneliness..
It seems that loneliness was all that life had to offer
But you rescued me
Took away the hurt that comes with pain
Made me a better me
Hurt...
Sometimes it would hurt so bad
Being alone and empty inside
Tears streaming down my face
And nowhere to run or hide
Clouds...
The clouds would hang over my head
Follow me everywhere I would go
With lightening and thunder crackling
And my head hung real low
Happiness...
But you took me to a world of happiness
To a place where everything's sweet
Washed away all my tears and sorrow
Had me shining from head to feet
Love...
Introduced me to a thing called love
Which you were happy to share
Held me tight and told me not to worry
Because you would always be there
Dreams...
My dreams of a life filled with love
Have now come true
I went from loneliness, hurt and stormy clouds
To a life of happiness, love and fulfilled dreams
When I was taken away by you

"Love is the magic carpet
That carries our hearts away into the horizon."

With You

I can
Feel
The thoughts
You think
When
You think
Of me
I can hear
You speak
When you
Whisper
My name
In
Your sleep
I can feel
Your joy
When I've
Made you smile
I experience
Your presence
Though between us
Are many miles
I
Am
With you

Lovers develop a bond, almost like telepathy.
Even when they are apart they are one in mind, body and soul

Thankful

Thanks for letting me find you
'Cause I've been searching the gardens where roses bloom
Looking for that flower that'll make my sky more blue
And more enjoyable for my eyes to view
I am so thankful
For the opportunity
That you have given to me
The privilege of getting close to thee
Exposing me
To the gleaming rays that emanate
From your inner beauty on which I concentrate
It's soothing for me to have met
That precious soul that stands so far apart from the rest
You're passing the test
And captivating my heart with finesse
I don't want to digress
Just want to progress
The path with your hand in mine
Together you and I
Could sail the shores of time
It's so divine
To know that I've
Stumbled upon a paradise
Where warm whispers of love
Melt the ice of
Loneliness that has chilled my soul for so long
Behold I'm no longer alone
For like a bird's song
My heart is happy to have found a home
To call its own
That's why I'm so thankful
So thankful for you

"Gratitude is the expression of a thankful heart."

Thoughts of You

In a world that's often unpleasant
Where joy can be hard to find
I feel a sweet refreshment
When thoughts of you fill my mind
And some days everything seems to be against me
The burdens so hard to bear
But the minute I picture you
The tension from a long day begins to rise like air
And sometimes after I've had a bad night
And awake unable to sleep
It's while hugging sweet thoughts of you tight
That I'm introduced to an inner peace
I don't know what my future may hold
But I'm sure I'll make it through
And in the midst of my struggles I'll remain bold
Strengthened by precious thoughts of you

"The gift of companionship is uplifting.
It gives hope in times of despair."

UNIMAGINABLE

Who could've known
What mind foreseen
That one would behold
The light of his own dream
Going within
Illuminating the soul
Putting warmth where there once was cold
Banishing caution
Relinquishing control
Unimaginable
And yet how can this be
That unaware and without alarm
An eruption exploded inside of me
I know that it's love
It shapes and it molds me
In the lonely hours it holds me
Completely unfolds me
Exposing
The most treasured and sacred things of my essence
It probes me
And becomes all that I want
That which I yearn for and need
Bringing joy into my life
A happy man am I indeed
A love with the strength
To compass me through and through
Reigning on the throne of my heart
Unimaginable
Yet so true

"Matters of the heart are mind-blowing at times."

Vacancy

I looked for you all day
But you weren't around
Then I realized
That you would be gone for a while
In spite of your absence I still had to smile
Just thinking of how
Foolish I must have seemed
Wanting to say something sweet
But was too nervous to speak
Guess I'm just weak
For a pretty girl whose eyes sparkle
Enough to bring light into a dark room
Hope I didn't startle you
With my nervous approach
Hope I wasn't being a pest, in letting you know
That I'm interested
In having you as the girl I begin my quest with
Manifested in the way I have no charm around you
And how I thank the Lord that I found you
I'm down for
Whatever you have to offer
And if there's a vacancy
In your life
Then I'm patiently waiting
To be in it
So your heart, I can tend it
With care
As a genuine friend
Who would always be there

"If there is a place in your heart for me...
I'd gladly reside there."

WAITING FOR YOU

Where are you?
I'm at the door of my heart
Waiting for you to come through
So what's the delay
And what price do I have to pay
To sway you my way
I count every day
We're not together a waste
So take
The steps that'll bring you straight
To my place
'Cause I can't wait
To see your face
And encircle your waist
With loving arms
That'll comfort and protect you from harm
Say yes and it's on
I'm ready to build something strong
Something above the norm
That'll last long
We could sing a love song
And over time develop a bond
As durable as iron
So don't waste no time
'Cause it's our time to shine
And we've got mountains to climb
To achieve what we've been anticipating
So come on...
I'm waiting

Procrastination is the grim reaper of opportunities

Waiting on Destiny

You could almost hear
My spirit quietly crying destiny
I'm at the point here
Where there's something specific I seek
In my heart I know
Although it's slow
That there's a fate designed for me
And it's a she
With a DNA structure
Tailored to entwine with mine
Whose heart won't puncture
The moment ours combine
Yes it's time
For the magic of love
To dazzle it way into my life
From above
Removing the strife
That I feel
The destiny I await
Is the thrill
Of becoming complete
Jagged emotions made straight
By the smoothness of unity
Can you feel me
I'm just waiting on destiny

"Everyone has a date with destiny.
You just have to recognize it when it comes."

Walk With Me

Walk with me
Through the tunnels of life
Hold my hand in the shadows
Rejoice with me in the light
Be my comfort and companion
When the trail becomes lonely
The treasure in my chest
Belonging to me only
Live with me, experience with me
The wonders and the bliss
Feel with me
The fire and the passion
Created when we kiss
Imagine with me
The endless possibilities
Of the pleasures we could attain
By fulfilling our fantasies
Dance with me
Hold my hand as we glide
Entangling to the rhythm
Together side by side

"The journey of life is better enjoyed with company."

WHAT I'VE BEEN MISSING

I awoke from a dream
Of you and me
A prophesy
Of upcoming things
And it was sweet
A pleasant treat
For my eyes to see
Now I believe
I've found my destiny
Or ours I should say
And I thank God for the day
That you came my way
I must say
To see your face
Was like Christmas day
What a gift!
And when you smiled
It made my heart skip
And my spirits lift
Just onc kiss
Is what I hope for
So I'll say my prayers
And wish upon a star
That you and I will go far
Not just the short distance
Cause baby girl
You're just what I've been missin'

"When you find someone that makes you happy,
The soul leaps for joy."

A Real Man

A real man
Is a man who shows others respect
He sees a woman
As more than an object for sex
He's not out for simply what he can get

A real man
Does his best to protect
His queen, offspring, and home
A real man doesn't roam
He's satisfied with his own

A real man
Isn't a player
Full of lies and games
He was taught to honor a woman
And never call her names

A real man
Is thoughtful and kind
He's not the average guy
Who appeals to the eye
But is empty inside

A real man
Is caring and considerate
He promotes his woman's growth
Instead of trying to hinder it

A real man
Won't degrade her
Or put her down
He won't lead her on
And then stop coming around

A real man
Doesn't take women for granted
He doesn't hop from woman to woman
Like a bunny rabbit

A real man
Is romantic
And creative in his love's expressions
He loves to pamper her
With gifts and warm affections

A real man
Is patient and understanding
He's gentle
And not demanding
He understands that she
Needs delicate and careful handling

A real man
Doesn't fight his girlfriend or wife
He doesn't get high
Unless it's the natural kind

A real man
Takes care of his responsibilities
He works diligently
To provide the needs of his family
He's strong, dependable, and sweet
He's what others can only pretend to be
But he's
The Real thing

"They don't make 'em like they used to."

Chapter 3

Enter His Gates (With Praise)

Lover of My Soul

He covers me
With His love
In ways you'd never dream of
Some see Him as judge
But I see Him as Abba Father
And everyday I look forward
To His warm embrace
And I long for the day
When I will behold His face
He shows His grace
With every breath that I take
And just when it seems that there is no way
You make a way
Where it seemed none could be made
And when I'm afraid
You comfort and console
Giving warmth when I am cold
Truly You are the lover of my soul

"The Lord is my Shepherd..."
-Psalm 23:1 (NKJV Version)

"The love of God is pure and unyielding"

I Believe

I believe
In the One who parted the Red Sea
The same One
Who called Lazarus out of a dead sleep
He said to me
That I would be lifted away
On judgment day
And brought to a place
Of golden streets where angels play
That's why I pray
And say His name in my heart's deepest most secret place
I believe anyway
Though I can't see your face visually
In my soul
I behold you spiritually
And I believe
You provide every breath that I breathe
I never go without
'Cause He provides all that I need
You planted the seeds
That became the Earth
And all that is seen
Is Your handiwork
The blessing and the curse
All stem from You
From the time of our birth
Our souls You pursue
You are the truth
And therefore I
Believe in You

"Through faith we see the unseeable,
And understand the unknown."

Son of a... King

Jehovah gave me this task
How can I fail
A million tears fell
To get me to where
I can finally prevail
A part of my life has been hell
But it took hell to turn my heart towards
Heaven's paradise
I used to not value life
But now it has no price
I see the light
Where once my vision was blind
I fell a thousand and nine times
But now I climb
Now I shine
'Cause I'm
A son
I come from the divine

"...as many as received Him, to them
He gave the right to become children of God,
To those who believe on His name"
John 1:12- (King James Version)

I See You

I saw You
The other day
There You were
You were that kind lady with the smile on her face
And I saw You this morning
When I opened my eyes
You were that feeling of joy
That I felt to be alive
And wow, I saw You
On my way to work
You were a beautiful flower
With her feet deep in the dirt
I saw You in church
As we lifted up praises
You were the joy that shined
On all Your children's faces
I saw You in places
I never thought I'd find
The mysterious and wonderful
God of all mankind

The world is a mirror reflecting God's image

In a painting, you don't see the painter...
but you know he was there.

Princely Presence

How can you hush
Greatness in the midst
How can you ignore that which
Is Heaven sent
How in the world do you turn a blind eye
When the presence of royalty shines
Right before your eyes
Bright as the sun rise
You've got to be blind
Or out of your mind
Not to comprehend
The power of a Prince
When he's in your midst
You've got to be slow
Not to know
Or at least be able to sense
The presence of a prince
When he's in your midst

"He came to his own,
And his own did not receive him."
John 1:11

My Shining Light

You're the shining light
That makes my life bright
And having you in my life is like
Ascending to the highest of heights
And now I see with new sight
And I just can't believe it's so right
Shining light you shine the way
Through my dark and lonely days
Finally I can turn the page
Of my life to reflect a better story
My heart you never neglect
And being with you is never boring
I'm soaring the skies on cloud nine
With you by my side
Shining so bright in my life

"I am the light of the world. He who follows me shall not walk in darkness, But have the light of life."

-John 8:12 (NKJV Version)

CAN YOU BELIEVE?

Can you believe
Creator of the seeds
And the trees
The Seas and all the things
That came into being
Can you imagine
A love that burns bright with passion
Unconditional no matter what happens
No matter your actions
Can you believe this tale
Someone to turn to when all else fails
When everyone has bailed
And left you stranded
A guiding hand
Through His commandments
Someone you can stand with
When the walls come crumbling down
There's a love to be found
No matter how bleak the situation
With grace that won't cease or get frustrated
A hand that will reach
To your lowest places
And sweep you higher than the sun
If you can believe...
Than your battle is already won

"Jesus said to him, If you can believe, all things are possible
To him who believes."
-Mark 9:23 (NKJV Version)

It's Your Choice

Where will you be when destruction hits
What will you be doing when the clouds split
And the Most Magnificent
Steps through the firmament
With the intent of pronouncing judgment
On the souls that spent their lives rebelling against
Him and His commandments
Hundreds of thousands of angels sent
To subpoena lost souls to the Courts of Justice
To be sentenced and given consequences
For every sin ever participated in
This is the end
And as a new era begins
Now where will you spend the ages as one who's eternal
Miserable in the burning aquatic inferno
Or in the glow
Of a paradise so wonderful
It's unexplainable
Where the streets are gold
And there's joy untold
Where nothing grows old
And the indescribable glow
Is the abode of fortunate souls
Made immortal
By the heavenly Father
So where will you be when death ushers you to the Other Side
Will your name be found written in the Book of Life
Today will you choose to obey
And inherit eternal twilight
Or will you do it your way
And be caught off guard when He comes like a thief in the night...
It's your choice

Eternity is a long time...
Choose wisely where you spend it

LAY ME DOWN

Dear Lord, when I lay me down to sleep
On my knees I pray
When I awake
It's to a place
And a better day
It's like my every breath is a waste
Cause here I am wasting away
Here on this Earth that You made
Everyday it's a race to get paid
Young men full of hate
Commit rape to get laid
That's why those bodies in graves
Got there because of AIDS
Young women
Keep sinning
Letting men get in their heads
Feed 'em what they wanna be fed
Just to get 'em in bed
Ain't nothing sacred no more
The rich just keep taking away from the poor
Building factories galore
They're called "sweat shops"
Got children working around the clock
Non-stop
Making shirts and designer socks
For those crooks at the top
Of the economic food chain
We look on T.V. and watch
But I promise you its not...a game
Dear God
Next time You lay me down to sleep
Resurrect me in one piece
To a world where there's peace
These things I ask Thee
As I lay me down to sleep

The most powerful weapon on Earth...
Is prayer

CASUALLY

Casually I enter
The depths of a web once weaved
Gliding through the minds
Of those not yet conceived
Landing on a plane
Unglimpsed by reality
With many onlookers
That seem alien to me
Feelings caught between
Fright and curiosity
Closer
And further I urge
To embrace
The Light before my eyes
Happy to be in this place
Away from the wails and cries
Happier even
From the joy that now upsprings
From the essence of my being
From the tunnels of my veins
And all of a sudden familiar
With a world I've never known
As if this is where I'm meant to be
As if I've made it home
At my place on the family tree
Totally one now with the Light
Effortlessly
Casually

DREAM HOME

I envision
A world
Devoid of hate
The capitol
Is love
Where peace
And kindness
Congregate
It's a place
So pure
And serene
The righteous
Dwell there
And
Their garments
Are clean
No sin
Nor reason to cry
And to the shackles
Of death
We've said good-bye
Hello to immortality
Liberty
And unimaginable fun
A world of hope
Where the terrors
Of the past are forgotten

"...I will dwell in the house of the Lord forever"
Psalms 23:6 (NKJV Version)

GODLY PRAYER

My God, my God
Respect fully emerges from me
I thank you for my creation, Your righteousness
And all Your mercy

I truly speak
As a loyal servant who
Would never turn his back
On a loving God like You

From the depths of the abyss
You arise like a bubble
Swiftly rescuing me
From all my troubles

Always on duty
Never ending is Satan's work
Smearing Your clean creation
With the foul smell of dirt

I must admit
Satan's won a lot of souls with his combat
But the souls of the righteous shall rejoice
While witnessing the great Lord's wrath

In the end Your Word shall prevail
That I know to be true
And nothing shall exist
Unless commanded by You

"Let us therefore come boldly to the throne of grace,
That we may obtain mercy and find grace
To help in time of need."
-Hebrews 4:16 (NKJV Version)

He's All I Need

All I need is my Lord
To sustain me in this land
To strengthen me through the storms
To lead me by His hand
He's all, all that I need
Though I was headed for destruction
You came and rescued me
He's all, all that I need
I was dead and in my sins
But then you died on Calvary
Now my life and all that I am
I give it all to thee
Because I'm nothing without you, Lord
You are everything I need
He's all, all that I need
Though I was headed for destruction
You came and rescued me
He's all, all that I need
I was dead and in my sins
But then You died on Calvary
When it seems like He's not there
And the trials they seem to get me down
I will look to the hills whence cometh my help
I know You'll place my feet on solid ground
Because He's all, all that I need
Though I was headed for destruction
You came and rescued me
He's all, all that I need
I was dead and in my sins
But then You died on Calvary

"The chief need of mankind
Is a relationship with his Creator."

In this life there is bitter
And sometimes sweet
Sometimes we cry
And other times are happy
It's like a roller coaster
With now consistency
I long for home
My home in the heavens way up high
Where joy does not appear one moment
Then vanish into the sky
It's a place where there will be no war
Nor shedding of blood
Where the growl of fear is hushed
By the soft hum of love
There are no famines or hunger
Gone are selfishness and greed
On the throne is the King of glory
He supplies all that His children need
One day my spirit will soar
Beyond the clouds of eternity
And all of us children of God
Will worship Him in love and harmony

"When Paradise is your destiny,
You get a little homesick sometimes."

Send 4 Me

Send 4 me...

A chariot of fire
Chauffeured by angelic drivers
Lift me higher
From the depths of my heart I inquire
Please fulfill my desire

Send 4 me...

Call me up to where you are
Past the stars
Beyond the moon and Mars
Deliver me from the wars and the scars
And times that are so hard

Send 4 me...

Carry me on eagle's wings
To a place only seen in dreams
Where golden streets meet crystal streams

Oh, send 4 me...

Because with You is where I'm meant to be

"In my Father's house are many mansions...
And if I go and prepare a place for you,
I will come again and receive you to Myself; that where I am,
There you may be also."
-John 14:2,3 (NKJV Version)

Lost Without You

Without You the world is doomed
Kids look gloom
As parents fight in the next room
You can hear the boom
As rockets fall from the sky
Raining fire
Devouring those who defy
Tears drop from homeless eyes
As the rich walk by
Ignoring their hungry cries
All lies
No truth in the pulpit
They need to stop it
Selling God's Word for profit
Today we need You in the worst way
The virus called AIDS
Sending millions to their graves
What a plague
Just like the days of Sodom and Gommorah
Destroyed by your wrath for living so whoreous
I bet You don't even know us
So far are we
From what you meant us to be
Must make You grieve
To behold our treachery
In blasphemy we laugh as we
Live oppositely
Of what You decreed
Obviously we're out of control
Bullets explode
And youthful souls

Never grow old
A mother's dreams implode
As her heart is lowered into the ground
She got the news and fell down
And her cry was the saddest sound
Today we need You in the worst way
Kids can't even play
Without getting sprayed with AKs
It's so crazy
Babies making babies
Then abort the fruit of their lust when
They realize they can't handle the repercussions
Of fornication
Some men crave for child molestation
Dear God we've strayed so far away from
Our place as a godly nation
Please deliver us from temptation
We'll never do it alone
'Cause on our own
We always go wrong
But all along
It's always been true
That with You there's nothing we can't do
But without You we're through
As the evidence overwhelmingly proves
We simply can't make it...
Without You

God is the light of the world
Without His guidance we stumble
And fall into darkness

Chapter 4

The Way of the World

A Girl Named Katrina

It isn't fair
Say a prayer with me
The wrath of God came alive in my city
Landslides, people died
They weren't ready
That girl Katrina was heavy
Hundred mile winds decimated the levees
Man it was scary
The way the waves of Ponchatrain
Smashed into our Big Easy
Like uppercuts to the brain
They said evacuate, and it wasn't a game
Now New Orleans is Atlantis
Might as well change the name
Cause it'll never be the same
And it's a shame
The way they left us stranded
We had incompetent leaders commanding
And it turned out tragic
Look at what happened
Radar and satellites in the sky
Described how the eye of a category five
Was in a direct line
To terrorize the shores of The Crescent
Yet with all that prior knowledge
They had no emergency plans present
To help those in need
Not everyone had the finances to leave
So many died in the streets
Or hungrily cried themselves to sleep
Praying for relief
From the stench of sewage and disease
I can't believe the response was so minimal
People dying on national T.V. --- it was critical
Nah, it was pitiful
Or maybe political

Whatever it was, how in the world can you ignore
Human beings going through hell right before
Your very eyes
Anchor man cried
Begging for assistance
But none came, and no one listened
Tears fell for loved ones missing
Shots rang out to let out the tension
In swarms they started looting
And if you were starving
That's the same thing you would be doing
The mighty Super Dome became a zone of polluting
Katrina caved the roof in
The situation was bleak
It was hard to breathe
And there was nothing to eat
Lights out wolves preyed on the weak
Women got raped, and lives were taken
With no authorities to bring order to the situation
It was frustrating
And that's an understatement
So where was Blanco and Ray Nagin
They looked like fools on the news
As far as what was going on
They didn't know what to do
Didn't have a clue
It took Geraldo Rivera to bring in the troops
So finally armed forces came to the rescue
They pulled a man off a roof
He was shivering cold with no shoes
What do you do
When everyone you love, and everything you owned
Including your home
Is gone
I feel so alone
So heart broken at this tragedy

It's unfortunate
I kept hoping it would never happen to me
Now my family
Are evacuees
In another state
It's like a foreign place
For everything gotta stand in line and wait
To get a plate
But thank God for the lives that were saved
May not be able to bathe
But at least you're not in a grave
Like so many are
Katrina came and hit us hard
Tore us apart
Into bits and pieces
And all we can do now is have faith and pray to Jesus
But I still can't believe it
The great City of New Orleans
Home of the French Quarter
Was underwater
And I thought couldn't nothing harm her
But in the end....
I guess we lacked the proper armor.

Dedicated to everyone who endured the wrath of Hurricane Katrina; In memory of all who didn't make it.

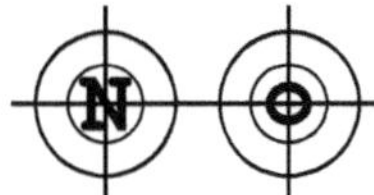
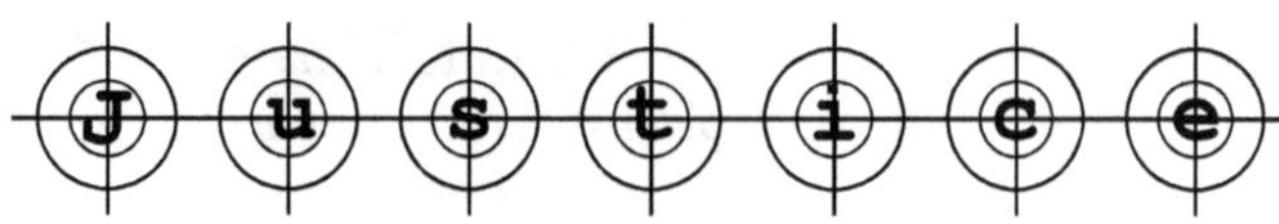

No Justice

There is no justice
Took my hand out and cuffed it
Behind my back
Took his billy club out and whack!
Across my back
And the tazer
Pierced my body like a laser
I convulsed
Upon the pavement
My pulse
Is slowly fading
These cops are full of rage when
Confronting Blacks
It is amazing
Pressing charges?
No they praised him
Gave him
A medal for bravery
For taking another vagrant
Off of the urban streets
And it occurred to me
That it's open season
On those who look like me
For any reason
Excessive force by police
Has come to be
The new form of lynching
Instead of hanging from trees
It's tazers, Glocks and M-16s
As mothers scream
From losing sons and daughters
In their young prime
They call it justified homicide
But in my mind
I'm thinking why
Is it justifiable
When I'm unarmed
And you have a rifle
I read in the Bible
That the love of mankind

Would grow cold
Using deadly force
On a child only 18 years old
At least you could've
Shot him in the leg
Instead of the head
Filled his body with so much lead
Where is the Justice
Where is the love which
You give your own family
But can erase one of my own
With a heartless mentality
This is insanity
How dare you
Expect us not to cause a ruckus
How long do you want us
To simply have discussion
When they're killing us
With no repercussions
There is no Justice
Only blue uniform wearing racists
Foot chases
Gun us down and give us cases
As the nation
Covers her eyes, so not to face it
And many Blacks are just complacent
But what happens when it's your Michael or Jason
Lying faceless upon the pavement

The Devil in Disguise

Sometimes the issues of life
Can explode in your face like
Grenades and dynamite
And though we'd like
For things to suffice and go right
At times the drama stage
Displays some shocking sights

Like learning your best friend's having an affair with your wife
Caught her leaving his house not once but twice
Now she was supposed to be taking classes at night
And that ain't right...
But man that's life

Like not thinking while drinking
And driving that night
Got arrested now facing your third felony strike
Now you didn't want to take the bartender's advice
But that's alright 'cause ...man that's life

Like crooked preachers
After service smoking reefer
In the back of the church
Putting in work on sister Keesha
Guess he's making her a believer
The world is full of deceivers
And that ain't right...but man that's life

Sort of like the terrible plight
Of crack-heads
Roaming the streets for days
Getting high
Trying to hide from all the failures they've made

And now a days
Young kids are growing up
Learning how to make a fast buck
Out there on the Ave swallowing ecstasy tabs
With 'gats tucked up in their guts
Now ain't that some sad stuff
Or maybe just some bad luck

But that ain't it
The darker the skin
The higher the chances of being discriminated against

We live in a society in which
The poor pay more taxes than the rich
Now tell me how does that make sense?
It doesn't...but that's the world we're living in

For instance
The night you and your family went out
And came home to find someone had broke in your house
Took everything except that old beat up couch
That's cold as ice...
But man that's life

Like when the angel with whom you jumped the broom
Became a demon soon after the honeymoon
And all that romance used to capture you
Transformed into commands, rules and attitudes
And now you're wondering how in the world can the two of you
Live together under the same roof
Doesn't sound too enticing right?
Well welcome to the marital life

Like when the people who seem so friendly
Turn out to be your most treacherous enemies

Listen to me
I'll tell you something about life that is true
Mistakes of your youth
For life can follow you
Like shadows of doom
No mercy, no reconciliation
Just labels and ostracization

In this nation
It's no longer undercover
Male on male lovers of one another
Referred to as the down low brothers

Don't it make you wonder?
Why you can't get a job because of nepotism
If you're not in the clique you can't enter the buddy system
It's capitalism...
Full of racism and sexism

And if you think that's a bad tradition
What about the babies discarded in trash cans
Or how that beautiful girl Mary Ann
Used to be a man

As con-men scam
The elderly unmercifully
Draining them of their social security

Young ladies submitting their purity
For acceptance in society

Satellites watch without cease
Trampling upon our right to privacy

They call it the beast
The all-seeing eye
The Apocalypse once prophesied
It's chaos and mayhem epitomized
But in my eyes...
Life ain't nothing but the devil in disguise

Life can be so wonderful...yet so painful at times

Signs of the Times

These are the signs of the times
Biblical lines
And everything that was prophesied
Has arrived
And transpires before our eyes
Morals dive
While destruction is on the rise
So many died
When the planes collided
On the 11th of September flames of war were ignited
Now it's all about vengeance
Tell me, is there an end to this
Cycle of devastation
Where compilations of bad creations
Like chemical agents
Stored in government basements
And atomic vibrations
Inject hate into the nations
Disasters shaken people's faith in
Him who made them
The light is growing dim
And the Earth's condition has taken a swim
In the cesspool of filth and destruction
Eruption of global destruction's
Got us all suffering
How disgusting that
Letters laced with anthrax
Triggered special-forces attacks
We went to war with Iraq
Due to terrorist threats
So soldiers get set
Prepare to meet the angel of death
As Mother Earth mourns her loss
Can't escape the nuclear Holocaust
It's Armageddon
The devil's wedding

It's sad when
Priests are undercover pedophiles
Draining life from young kids like insects carrying West Nile
It's wild how
Spies trained for espionage
Are stealing secrets, selling lies
And playing both sides
Murder rate going high
Like the Star Trek Enterprise
Our demise
Is due to a debase mentality
What kind of place
Will embrace perverse sexuality
We must be crazy
And even economically we suffer defeat
That is, everyone but the elite
Who creep upon their victims like savage animals
Those thieves
All ways involved in some corporate corruption scandal
Turn the channel
Cause the news makes me sick
All it shows is how the world's filled with hatred
Serial rapists catching felony cases
Meanwhile smiling faces disguise hearts that are racists
Give me a break from this
Environment of souls that are frozen cold
Since the days of old
These events have been foretold
But now they're happening
And it's evident
That we're living in...
The Signs of the Times

With the decline of morals,
Values, and respect for human life, it seems
We're on the path to self-destruction

History's Miseries

Imagine a world filled with drama
Since the beginning of time
Evidence in archaeological finds
Reminds us that we're living in the ending of time
Time lines define
Armies guided by imperial minds
Behind all the glory
And sugar-coated stories
Lurk blood thirsty kings
Lead by greed
Who couldn't sleep
Unless they conquered another man's land
Unsatisfied with what they had
Soldiers were used as pawns to expand
The interests of those in the palace
Rhetorical speeches infected the hearers with malice
As they marched on
From the plains of Babylon
Ruled by Sargon
To the conquests of Philip of Macedon
Carried on
By his son Alexander
Commander
Of the Greek fleet
He...
Swept the Persians off their feet
Then died mysteriously
Then the Romans entered the scene
Waging war from Egypt to the Black Sea
Made it all one community
Pretty soon you see
That history repeats
In cycles of adversity
Whether Hitler in Germany

Or Crips and Bloods settling beef
On LA streets
Trigger happy police
Use force excessively
Japanese against Chinese
Arab against Israeli
No peace in the Middle East
Or Afghanistan
Terrorized by Osama and his clan..the Taliban
Civilization is simply a scam
Disguising a world wide campaign
Of tyrants engaged in a game
Where they use us as puppets to maintain
Their reign
But it's the little people who get the saddest treatment
While the so called elite
Live a life of luxury
Its something
How history can be
Such an ugly sight to see

Listen to the Silence

Can you hear
The vibes in the atmosphere
So loud and clear
When you use your third ear
To perceive
What's underneath the surface of reality
Which leads me to believe
There's more to be seen
Than what it seems
What I mean
Is certain activities happening globally
Are simply a scheme to deceive
To create a mass breed of seeds
Dependent upon the powers that be
For everything
And logically
There's no such thing as being free
That's something that has never existed
That concept is just a twisted
Layer of illusion
Used in
The campaign to bring confusion
As a bind upon the minds of all mankind
If you could rewind time
I'm sure you'd find
That the conspiracy
Was implemented intricately
Over a period of centuries
Dispensed in a series
Of atrocities affecting everything here
Life itself is shedding tears
And fear is real
In hearts and minds far and near
Does any one hear
The vibes in the atmosphere
So loud and clear
But only when you use your third ear
For the voice of truth is silent
Amongst the roar of lies, deception, and violence
So listen to the silence

Pay attention; it's often what's not being said that says the most

INNER DEMONS

I see broken hearts
Painted red with lies and abuse
Encased in lives
That hide and recluse
So many use smiles
To disguise their true roots
But try as you may
There's no escape from the truth
Tender eyes
Confide the mind of a savage
Who's weary and tired
From carrying piles of baggage
So hard he tries
To disappear like black magic
But in time he realizes
The demons have caused so much damage
It gets to the point
Where he just can not stand it
And in an instant
A weapon is brandished
The news flashes
A crime that is gruesome and tragic
He went to work one last time
To let them all have it
Finally managed
To get his 15 seconds of fame
He went out with a bang
To his very own brain
And it's a shame
He never told a soul
How the demons kept calling his name

In memory of Columbine High and Virginia Tech

Grave Loss

Lightening flashes
Before the thunder
Gunfire, blade gashes
Flood waters pull faces under
And so I wonder
Slumber as I struggle to believe this
To find the answer doesn't take a genius
AIDS and SWAT raids
Plague the days like cancer
Air waves congested
Pollution's destroying the solar plexus
Like Smith and Wessons
On the hips of adolescents
If life is a learning lesson
Then I guess we've failed to get the message
And no one's protesting
Guess we've learned to accept it
To the sky my eyes keep checking
When will He emerge
In the clouds like the birds
Declaring the Words
That will correct all wrongs
And bring us out of this zone
Of Darkness
And back to the hope, because we've lost it
We've utterly lost it

Aside from your soul
The most valuable possession one can lose
Is hope

UNFIT CRITICS

I arise like a phoenix
From the ashes of my blackness
No longer held captive
Or out-casted
By double standards
In a society where
The same ones who point and stare
Are the same ones who breathe the same air
As I do
But I'm no fool
The things you condemn me for... you do them too
Or even worse
Evil doers in closets lurk
Wearing shiny suits to cover their dirt
The truth hurts
When exposed
Judge Levinworth sentenced me
For selling the same dope he sniffs up his nose
Now ain't that cold?
But that's how it goes
In the white collar criminal code
Elected officials paint their pockets gold
With tax dollars they stole
To the highest bidder their soul goes
While the real issues get put on the back burner stove
And I'm the criminal!?
Well at least I'm not hypocritical
Throwing rocks and hiding your hand
So called priests more woman than man
Pillars of the community with perverted and blood stained hands
I don't understand
How you criticize
Sanitize your own lives
Before you try to judge mine

On the outside you shine
But deep inside
You're the filthiest grime
Behind a disguise you hide
Mr. District Attorney
For my harmless crime
You tried to burn me
But what about the late night creeps
Into your child's room as he sleeps
And what about your addiction to child pornography?
Take heed, oh masters of deceit
When you point the finger at me...
Back at you is pointing three

"Let he that has no sin cast the first stone"
--Jesus Christ

It's Time to Change

Our current state's a disgrace
Frown on my face
As I meditate upon our fate
In every way we've embraced
A life of servitude on another's estate
Why fight for crumbs when you can bake your own cake
It's idiotic when you think about it
You tell people the truth and they still doubt it
Revolutionaries shouted with force for the cause
Shed their blood, even died to change the laws
But they suffered and died in vain
Sacrificed their all
Yet the men of today don't even know their names
And that's a shame
It's not a game to smile and laugh at
What can be so funny
When our neighborhoods are infested with crack
Destroying our lives like exposure to anthrax
And it's a fact that being black means you're under attack
And the worst enemies, your own kind
And at this rate of genocide
We don't have a long time
To repopulate the United States
No wonder Latinos have replaced us as the minority race
Awake or attend you own wake
Now's the time for us to educate
Ourselves so that we can be great
No longer grim statistics in society
No longer the majority of those in poverty
And I believe that we can be
Superior figures in every industry
Do you know it's in our genes to achieve
Do your own history
We descended from kings and queens

Have we forgotten what that really means
What it means is that we're royalty
And that it's in us to succeed
If we apply ourselves there's no boundary we can't exceed
Knowledge is the key
So that's what we need
Stop calling yourselves niggers because what you speak
Shows what you believe yourselves to be
Right now our future seems bleak
But we can change directions and head for victory

The wise evolve, the fool revolves

Praying for a Better Day

Lost and tossed
Like waves in the sea
Brains turned off
By the toxins we breathe
Can't sleep
Let alone think intellectually
It's deep
How we let ourselves
Be used and abused
Alarms ringing like bells
And still we play the role of confused
Animated pieces of flesh
Partially alive
But with minds that bare the image of death
Black holes swallowing souls
While corruption
And weapons of mass destruction
Disintegrate and permeate
Creating such an altered state
Of what used to be
Look at our society
It's wicked and polluted
And flooded with filth
Morals and principles have been diluted
To the point where we do wrong and feel no guilt
How can we say that there's a heart in our chests
We hurt each other as our forefathers turn in their graves and can't rest
Man that's cold
We've been sold and enslaved again
You would think that one knows
How not to go somewhere they've already been
Can't begin to comprehend
What motivates us to be this way
Wish it would end
I pray for judgment day
So children can go out and play
Without lead flying their way
And all races can congregate
In love and not hate....
I'm just praying for a better day

May the dark and dismal hours of desolation
give way to the bright and radiant dawn of a new day

JUST THINKING

Sometimes I think about things
Like how the world's changed
And how we've flushed our morals
Down the drain of sorrows
Our tomorrows forever tainted
With the sins of the past
What a picture we've painted
How long will it last
Before the deadly crash
The world's vehicle is heading toward
I wonder was life really meant to be so hard
Or have we made it this way
These are the things that I contemplate
And the reason I pray
I'm seeking a way to understand why
It hurts just to open my eyes
And be alive
Deep inside I sense and realize
It's not supposed to be like this
The Earth used to be paradise
Full of joy and bliss
The only paradise now belongs to the rich
It's wrong to insist
On going in this
Wrong direction
We should hold an election
And let the selection
Be the principles
We used to uphold
Long ago
So we can grow as a people
No longer shackled by petty prejudices

Like different colored skins
We could all be friends
And try to make amends
And wash away the sins
Of the past with the suds of forgiveness
And rise above all the childish bickering
Cause the only difference in
My origin and yours
Is the different wombs we explored
To exit the flesh pit
But in a realer sense
All our souls began within
The mind of the same Spirit
Do you feel it?
It's the truth, so open your ears to hear it

Positive change starts in the mind as a thought
Then bursts into the world as action

SINSATION

Must I bleed to breathe
Must my mothers grieve
And what's the need
Of such life loss
Through greed we've paid the price cost
As the wages of our rebellion
Make our lives a living hell when
Money, drugs, and sex
Are indicators of success
And it's
Considered best
When a woman wears less
And look how many necks
She turns
But is a moment of flesh
A good enough reason to burn
Or forfeit your soul
For high priced cars
But nobody knows
Just how far
Down the road of degradation
We've traveled
Sin is a sensation
We all have to battle
Not give in to
When evil tempts you
Remember, you are a temple
Not something simple
So use your head...
Because the battle is mental

The will to do what's right
Is a bridge over the turbulent waters of temptation

The Answerless Question

I visualize
Through a wise pair of eyes
Amazed that I'm
Still alive
In these perilous times
Surprised I even made it this long
In a city that's really a war zone
Iraq and them
Ain't got nothing on the ghettos I've been around
Where shot bodies
From black on black possees
Can be found all around
And here I am trying to expound
On an answerless question
How did we get from
Slavery to being a deadly weapon
To our very own brethren

The answer's out there, but we're missing it

What Happened

What happened to the Malcom X's and Martin Luther Kings
The Rosa Park's and boycotting
The "I Have a Dream"s
And marches with crowds that sing
"We Shall Overcome"
Civil rights won by those who wouldn't run
But fought like Ghandi
Non-violently against inequality
What happened to the protests and arrests
For refusing to settle for less
And demanding respect
What happened to the Huey Newtons
And youths who induced revolutions
Finding solutions
To problems we'd been subdued to
What happened to the Marcus Garvey's
Bob Marley's and Black Panther Parties
Who prowled the streets
Protecting their peeps
From bandits in sheets
What happened to the Toussaint L'Overtures
Who'd rather face death
Than be suppressed anymore
What happened to the Harriet Tubmans
And underground get-aways
On trips that made
Free men out of slaves
What happened to the Fredrick Douglasses
Who exposed slavery's evil for what it is
What happened to the Chaka Zulu's
And fierce warriors who
Fought nail and tooth
What happened to the Nelson Mandela's
Inventors and trend-setters

What happened to "Right On" and "self-pride"
Parties all night long
Where nobody died
What happened to showing respect to our women
Instead of degrading them with no limit
What happened to educating our minds
So we could excel, not be behind
Or confined
To modern day plantations
With all our rights stripped away from us
I seriously think it's time to discuss
What exactly it is...that has happened to us

Blood, sweat and tears paved the way
For us to be where we are today,
May we never forget the sacrifices that were made for us

The Hood Ain't Good

The path I traveled
Landed my life in battles
And conflicts in the bricks
Where scandalous chicks with tricks
Will blow you a kiss
Then set you up by their clique
Been in the mix since the age of six
Hit the block with a nose full of snot
In my high-tops
Watching the homies tote slingshots
Slinging snowdrops
How can you stop
Your life from sliding down the drain
When all you've ever witnessed was pain
On streets ran by gangs that spit flames
Creating thunder without rain
You had to learn game to maintain
In a jungle with so many predators
United ghettos of America
Where only the strong survive
The weak lose their lives
Cross your T's and dot your I's
Or kiss your life good-bye
Chalk lines show the signs
Of the Reaper
Etched out in the street
Dude looked like a sleeper
In a permanent sleep
Black SUV's
Driven four deep
Packed with heat
And ready for beef
So clear the streets when the sweeper sweeps
'Cause when they spit

They don't care who they hit
Just ask the innocent
Occupiers of graveyards
Bandana'd faces spray from stray cars
To prove that they're hard
Them old folks pray hard
For a generation gone astray
Scrappin' in the streets barefeet
Is how we played everyday
Crack pipes and razorblades
Lace the ally ways
Dime sacks and dollars trade
To blaze them Mary Jays
Dice games in hallways
Gotta hustle to get paid
The ghetto is our cage
That's why we stay
And that's just a typical day...
Around my way

The voice of the ghetto cries out in pain
Begging for change

Voice of the Ghetto

Listen to a tale
Follow as I lead you through a trail
Of deaths, drug sets and sub techs
Where the wrong color could get you wet in a sec
Check the scene
Black juveniles chasing C.R.E.A.M.
Seventeen and strapped to the teeth
Serving fiends
Dodging jackers and them crooked police
With no peace
For them old folks that be trying to get sleep
Them you girls creep
Get turned out by neighborhood O.G.s
Then hit the scenes
Tricking for P.I.M.P.s
With low self-esteem
Where can we go with no dream
No vision for a better future
To used to
Having it bad in life
And they wonder why
We don't have our piece of the pie
Due to a lack of academic appetite
Mom said "Go get a job"
But Shorty replied "nah"
"Them people ain't actin' right"
He'd rather go and jack at night
Camouflaged in black and strapped up tight
On a mission to go and snatch sellers of that pearly white
A few snorts to get hype
Enroute to the target on bike
But the cat must've been psychic
'Cause as soon as the door got kicked
That's when the Mack 10 spit
And them hollow tips went in...
The beginning of a tragic end
And it don't make sense
Listen
Let me take you on an expedition
To tenements with no air condition

Where tears glisten
On a young face who hasn't eaten in days
Hasn't seen his mom in days
And yeah she got paid
But she smoked it away
Now her legs she's gotta spread
For Johns and married Toms who stray
From the burbs to the hood
To participate in the trade
Of cash for human goods
We're under a curse
But nobody's trying to break the spell
Authorities pull up in a black and white hearse
To bury the living dead in jail
Some say the ghetto's a living hell
Here on Earth
It's like running on treadmills in reverse
We're putting in work, but on the wrong ones
The real enemies supply us with guns
And we run to accomplish their means
Disintegrating self
Over cities and streets named after Europeans
Now either we're too naive
Or just unwilling to see
That we've been programmed
To make our own selves extinct
And it don't make sense
Welcome to the hood
I'm your tour guide
Now sit back, relax and enjoy the ride
As I
Paint for you the picture of a nightmare
Where
Street soldiers engage in guerrilla warfare
It's all clear
Man is a product of his environment
But what happens when
His environment
Is full of violence
And little time is spent
Rearing him

Single moms struggling to pay the rent
And with no guardians present
Children band together in rebellious adolescence...
The natural progression to the criminal elements
Everyone's guessing
"What's the problem with our youth"?
To tell you the truth
They need someone to talk to
To prepare them for life
'Cause all mom and dad did was fight every night
Leaving the tykes confused about what's wrong or right
Wonder why lil Judy had five kids before she made 18
Never told she was a queen
And the love and affection she didn't receive at home
She found in the arms
Of men willing to sing the right songs
Just as long as they could have their way
Then they were gone the next day
Left her all alone to carry the weight...
A single mom pregnant with AIDS
We're living in the Biblical days
Before our very eyes unfold
Everything the scriptures foretold
Bloodshed and misery covers the globe
The Earth is posed
In self-destruction mode
Con-men in suits use religion to cloak
Their true motives
They're preying on folk's emotions
So their pockets can grow swollen
From collection money that's stolen
Deep as the ocean
Is the abyss of our sins
What began in the garden hasn't ended since
And it don't make sense

Awake, or attend your own wake

REDIRECTION

My approach may be unorthodox
But the vocals and penmanship I drop
To get my people off the block
Off the rocks
Sitting ducks, just waiting for the cops to stop
Frisk ya from locks to socks
What ya got in stock
One false move...pop! pop!
Man it's like that box
With the carrot in it
When you enter it drops
And your behind is finished
Beware of the gimmicks that trick the senses
Brand name clothes and stores
Rob you of your riches
There's nothing wrong with dressing nice
And rocking designer kicks
Or riding fly in fresh whips
But see the problem arises
When you line another's pockets
Before addressing the topic
Of self-profit
Unwise economics empty out your wallets
What's the logic in rocking gold watches
And you're living with moms in the projects
I'm not trying to knock it
My object is to broaden your horizons to better options
Soldiers redirect your focus
We're disappearing like hocus pocus
Faces painted on posters
Now how are we 'gonna rise to the occasion
How are we 'gonna find ways to make ourselves a stronger nation
Caught in material fascination
"Bling-bling" salivation
Use your imagination
It's what you see that leads to captivation
Fishermen use bait when they fish
Same tactics on us they practice
In front our eyes be flashing
Expensive cars, jewelry and fashion

But ain't no jobs to make it happen
So you 'gotta sell crack and
Go jacking
Each other blasting
While they sit back laughing
Judge waiting to take action
Give you the max and
Send you up-state where nothing but time be passing
To the podium I step to address this session on redirection
Any questions?
Then peep the lessons my vocal chords are manifesting
Financially we're stressing
And I'm guessing
'Cause we're neglecting self-investment
400 billion pesos we disburse annually
But what hurts is we don't see
Non of it reach
Back to our community
And economically that affects you and me
Where does our money go
In what do we place our hope
Let me know
'Cause we can't grow
Acting rich while living poor
'Cause ain't none of us balling out of control
Until we all do it as a whole
Owning our own stores
Mining our own gold
King Solomon bank roll
With Nasdaq on hold
Not just with money, but setting goals
And accomplishing
Better living for us...'cause that's what time it is

In order to change destinations
You've got to change directions

When Angels Cry

They're selling dirty laundry on talk shows
Springer and Maury
Profit from the hurtful seeds that others sowed
Pool souls expose
Every problem and sin
There they go fighting on national T.V. again
Audience laughing while the hosts and producers go cashing in
Filling their pockets with the pain and tears of their guests
Ratings soar to the sky when a bra is stripped off a chest
It entertains us
But what happens to them when we turn off the set
It's pure neglect
To taunt and mock the agony of our fellowman
To kick him while he's down
Instead of offering a helping hand
Do we even give a damn?
Certainly not,
From what my eyes see
Only when its on our doors that tragedy knocks
Do we take it seriously
Then we look for a shoulder upon which to cry
How hypocritical, when the same sentiment to others we deny
Angelic cries pierce the sky
And the question I keep asking
Is where has the love went
The world is bent
Out of shape
And in a race
To embrace suicide
Babies coming out the womb yelling "do or die"
As angels cry

'Cause we were made in the image of deity
But live oppositely
Of what we were meant to be
Demonic groupies
Refusing to live righteously
There's got to be a solution
To this infusion of genocide
And some way to stop the flow of tears
From the angel's eyes

For every soul that suffers and hurts, an angel sheds a tear

A Call to Action

How are we gonna climb the stairs
If we're psychologically impaired
Or scared
To kindle the flames of revolution
Lets get together and develop solutions
Start flooding the universities as students
Becoming affluent
In the fundamentals of our society
Including the laws of domestic and foreign policy
In this world we can't afford to be ignorant
Because ignorance equals a lack of inner strength
In a world where knowledge is key
Illiteracy means you can not compete
Only with understanding can we seize opportunities
Never allow yourselves to be
Blind and in the dark
While your opponents are
Crafty and smart
It's time to start
Magnifying our brain power
Pouring over books for hours
And making our voices louder
Than what they now are
In order to promote and defend our cause
With strength and diligence
Putting an end to the passage of biased laws
Herein is a call to action
It's time for intellectual expansion
If we ever hope to graduate from our sad estate
Let's correct past mistakes
And pave the way
For better days

For us in the USA
They say life is 90% of how you handle situations
When you face a problem, either you fight or run away from
What stands in the way of your destination
Be it economics or education
Social assimilation
Or the hope for liberation
Either way, it's time for advancement
Herein is a call to action
It's time to display some determination and passion
And begin to elevate in every fashion

Ignorance blinds, knowledge empowers,
Action accomplishes

Better Outcome in Mind

Plateaus and landscapes
Criss-cross my mind
Spreading like drapes
Playing thoughts in time
Rewind to find
And correct the errors I've made
Thought I was scheming but I'm the one who got played
But I stayed with high hopes
Although life had me against the ropes
It's hard to cope
When the world you thought you knew
Seems to have declared war on you
And here I am with no army or troops
In a state of mute
Although they say freedom of speech
The enlightened few
Know we really aren't free
If we are then why does the government monitor our every move
With satellites and tracking devices
Can't even tie your shoes
Without it going into a database
Got me wanting to disappear without a trace
Escape covertly
Find my real family tree
Expand my genes
Teach them what life really means
And go to my grave realizing at least some of my dreams

Blasphemy

Head bowed, I blink
As I think of the condition we're in
In the muck we continue to sink
As if there's no end
Tears slide from my eyes
In memory I envision the
Days gone by
When a continent
And the color of our skin
Was the binding tie
That kept us united
But then we got divided
And didn't try to fight it
Until it was too late
Now here we are...
Strangers in a strange place
What a waste
We came from dynasties
Where kings ruled with queens
And empires
That spread knowledge like fire
That minds would come from afar to acquire
A glimpse of the intellect
That we possessed
It makes me upset
To see how far we've digressed
From what used to be our destiny
Our present day reality's
So far from our ability
It's killing me
To see how we've passionately
Become our own enemy
Makes no sense to me
We're in the same boat with now paddle
Everyone knows it takes numbers to go to battle
Yet we're out numbered

Because our anger is often aimed at our peers
Instead of the corrupt forces that have haunted us for over 400 years
Who faked
Stole, and raped
Enslaved
Then built a nation that never paid
The slaves who made it great
Then they began to hate us
Tried to segregate us
Yet in God they trust
What?
What a joke that was
Flood our neighborhoods with drugs
Then lock us up for selling our own people a poisonous buzz
Know what it does
It burns the brain cells
Turns the body into a walking jail cell
It's hell but it's fair
Got us on welfare
But they've got it made in the shade
So why should they care
We need to stop and stare
'Cause the only way we'll ever go any where
Is if we wake up and see
That the enemy isn't you and me
We need to grasp the concept of unity
Or we'll stay in defeat
And always be beat
Stop the cycle or become deceased
Because the real tragedy
Isn't what was done to you and me
But that we've allowed it to be
And that to me
Is blasphemy

"Stand together...or fall apart."

Check Yourself

It seems my dreams
Never materialize
So many times
Watched them vanish before my eyes

But I still maintain
Cause in my mind frame...
That's just a part of the game

So used to feeling pain
That it's a common thing
And the way we live
It's like we're going insane

Because a lot of what we go through
Is self-imposed
And even though it's true
They flood the 'hood with coke
But we're the ones who chose to sniff it in our nose

And sure, they're building all these jail cells
But who the hell's committing crimes and turning in ourselves?

The scales of justice aren't balanced right
So why not stay out of that blind trick's sight?

That's common since
But when you tell people this
They take offense

I don't know why I keep hoping
That people will one day open
Their eyes and realize
That they're the reason why we've got it bad in life

Guess may be it helps
To blame somebody else
But if that's true then they control you
Cause can't nobody make you do
What you don't want to do

So let's be real here
And if the picture isn't clear
I'll make it clearer
The one you need to check, son
Is the reflection in the mirror

Success and failure is controlled
By the owner and operator of your life...you!

Get Serious

The world exists
But there's more to it
Than ghetto lingo
There should be more to a flow
Than money, guns and dope
Instead of giving hope
They're rhyming about who they gone smoke
And the whip they drove
When they went to the show
While brothers going for broke
And catching cases imitating stories somebody wrote
Just didn't know
That's its fictional
Most of it studio
If rappers did the things they wrote
They would spend most of their time in court
But nope
It's all about the record sales
Luxury hotels
And making pockets swell
By fabricating gangsta tales
Meanwhile we're catching all kinds of hell
Wasting our lives in jails
So let me tell you what we've got to preach
Messages that speak
Of more than just the city streets
Ya see
We need to teach this misguided generation
With lyrics that instruct on how to rise in this United Station
Knowledge is liberation
But ignorance and violence perpetuate Black frustration
It takes our minds away from
Our need
To lay aside hatred and jealously

We're on the same team
So why be enemies?
Rappers, the words you plant are seeds
And the effect will either be
Negative or positivity
We already have more destruction than we really need
But if we come together we could be
Kings and Queens in our communities
Rap is a voice so teach
The message lyrically..
Seriously

Leadership is a gift, a responsibility
That should never be taken for granted

Time Will Tell

Time is a very mysterious element
It has been known to heal and mend the wounds
Inflicted by this cruel and merciless place
It can remove the bitterness from the bitter
Put a smile on a frowning face
Change a person who only knows evil
One who rapes and steals innocent souls
Instill mercy and love in his heart
Have him shining like a block of gold
Take the anger from within a mad man
Put love into a loveless heart
Bring peace to a feuding couple
Open the gates to a brand new start
You see, life can be like a fairy tale
With the hands of time on your side
It can change you in many, many ways
Either open or close your eyes
But the hands of the clock aren't always lenient
They can also be dreadfully mean
You can find yourself in a heap of trouble
Doomed to live your scariest dream
I've seen many lives shattered
During various spans of time
Seen thousands of souls perishing
Still the murder rate continues to climb
Me, myself, I want to end destruction
But can I plead with the hourglass?
On my knees before father time
Begging for peace at last
No, I truly doubt it
Father time takes orders from no one
He's really very stubborn
Doing things as he wants them done

Life can be a joyous experience
Like a soft melody in your ear
But if you don't use time wisely
You might wish you were never here
The question is...What does life have in store for me?
Will I fight with all my will
Or will I become a victim
Defeated on the battlefield
Will I prosper in this life
Will all things work out well
Or am I doomed to inevitable destruction
The answer...
Only time will tell

Time is the key
That can unlock the door to your destiny

When Will It End?

The saga continues
Like the wind that blew
From the spinning of the revolving door
Blind-folded souls with no goals
Travel the same roads as before
I wonder but can't imagine
What could be so tempting about self-mutilation
When will we realize
Or focus our eyes
On the fact that we're more than we perceive ourselves to be
What the next man thinks
Doesn't define our reality
But is it our complexion
Or lack of affection for one another
That's got us crowding the jails and sleeping in the gutter
I just want to know where we went wrong
What on Earth could inspire one to kill his own
I don't understand
Even the caveman
Knew he had to stick with his clan
Not disband
But somehow
The basics evade us
Then and now
We've always lacked trust
We're so lost
With hearts as cold as frost
And ears stopped to the message that was preached
If we just tried
We could get our people off the streets
And become players
On the court that matters
The saga continues
But only because we allow it to
At any point we could change
Break the cycle and maintain
But it's up to us to do so
Liberate yourselves my people
You have the keys to unlock the door!

If life is a learning lesson, we've failed to grasp the message

Unjust Satisfaction

It's bigger than what we see
It's bigger than you and me
Bigger than the he economy
It's bigger than Trump or Hillary
We haven't a clue as to what's actually reality
Propaganda brainwashes our mentality
Whatever they want us to believe...
They just put it on T.V.
And we accept it blindly
How naive
To so eagerly receive
Those viruses into our mainframes
They were designed to contain
To put our minds in chains
We're not a threat if we can't use our brains
And that's the aim
To keep us tame
Citizens that take orders and listen
But never question the system
Or fight to better conditions
Why waste time being an activist
When there's so much to be distracted with
Valuable time spent
On insignificance
The answer's out there but we're missing it
Too busy getting rich
Or using drugs to quench
An inner itch
With broken spirits that need to be fixed
And emotions that are mixed
With the spirit of lust
Women used as toys to please us
We live in an over-sexed society

Everywhere you look it can be seen
In magazines
Plastered on every screen
A movie won't sell without a steamy scene
Commercials with women in tight jeans
Internet pornography's
Destroying marriages by the scores
As husbands reject their wives for whores
Adult stores
Frequented more than churches
My heart hurts and I wonder if its worth it
Are we satisfied with where our Earth is?

Complacency is the father of destruction

UNSATISFIED

I'm at the point in my life
Where something just has to give
I'm just so weary, exhausted,
And disappointed with the way that it is
With the way that I live
I'm so tired of the same dull,
Unproductive lifestyle
Environment of shady individuals
Doing nothing worthwhile
Nothing worth a smile
And so I'm ready for new horizons
And new people
An escape from these pit vipers
So full of evil
And so deceitful
Therefore I seek a better vicinity
A life with more productivity
And less dramatic activity
I'm unsatisfied with this existence
So I'm seeking a better lifestyle to enlist in
With a new and improved frame of mind
I've been gifted
Now I need some better shoes
To try and fit in
Where can you go
To shake these destructive people and bad attitudes
Wake up in the morning
Ugly faces staring back at you
So sad but true
On every side
A confrontation with negativity,
Counter-production, ignorance,
And stupidity,

Illiteracy, and foolish souls
Who are unproductive
Lost minds so corrupted
And self-destructive
I'm so disgusted to cohabitate
With people so full of hate
And so ungrateful
Their thirst for self-hurt so insatiable
Time after time
Selfishness and warped minds
Walking around with shut eyes
Terrified and blind
Content with being lazy, stagnated, and confined
And yet I rise amongst the dead people
Knowing inside that for me there's a sequel
To this messed up condition
I'm unsatisfied so I strive to amplify my existence
'Cause this here's ridiculous
And I wonder if it's all a bad dream
Got me surrounded by zombies and primitive thinking
Scumbag excuses for human beings
How cruel it seems
I'm unsatisfied
With this existence
So I seek a better lifestyle
To enlist in
A new and improved frame of mind
I've been given
Now I desire
A better world to live in
And what's got me trippin'
Is how these backward cavemen
Want nothing for themselves
And try to take others to the grave with them
But I refuse to be a victim of that system
What a sad world I envision

There's 'gotta be more to it
Than this lack-luster life devoid of love
Of which unfortunately
I'm the unproud owner of
It always was my quest in life to pursue
An enjoyable, more rewarding place to take root
And to reach that end
I'll harness every effort, mental power, and strength
To apprehend my ideal atmosphere
I'm like an ant on the ground
Looking up at the clouds and stratosphere
Wishing I could climb the sky
On wings of agility
Until I fulfill my dreams
Of physical, mental,
And spiritual stability
Because this life for me
Is unsatisfactory
I'd rather be in another galaxy
Far away from the tragedies,
Catastrophes, and lies
I'm sick and tired of being sick and tired
And so I rise
And continuously strive
To reach the greener pastures of the other side

Your out look on a situation
Determines how it affects you

What Will It Take?

They say the best way to hide something from us Blacks
Is in a book
In life there are many roadmaps
If you just look
We could charter the same paths the prosperous took
It's sad but indifference to knowledge has got us shook
I wonder why
Our forerunners died
To provide us with opportunity
But what they coveted we reject, and that's lunacy
And if this persists we're doomed to be
The proletariats of industrialized countries
Firmly disbarred from positions where we run things
We fail ourselves if we continue in this descent
Down the dark and dismal realm of ignorance
Makes no difference
What the color of our skin is
My main concern is the condition of our existence
We're not even trying to correct our mistakes
Instead of growing stronger together we cultivate hate
And advocate the perpetual oppression of our race
Although others take part we also participate
By falling for the traps put in place
To make sure we never elevate
Yet I pray for the day
When we'll awake from our slumber
And start doing our best to help each other
Instead of holding one another under
I just wonder...
What will it take
To liberate...
The Black race

Some questions
Only God has the answer for

TIME TO CHANGE

Our current state's a disgrace
Frown on my face
As I meditate upon our fate
In every way we've embraced
A life of servitude on another's estate
Why fight for crumbs when you can bake your own cake
It's idiotic when you think about it
You tell people the truth and they still doubt it
Revolutionaries shouted with force for the cause
Shed their blood, even died to change the laws
But they suffered and died in vain
Sacrificed their all
Yet the men of today don't even know their names
And that's a shame
It's not a game to smile and laugh at
What can be so funny
When our neighborhoods are infested with crack
Destroying our lives like exposure to anthrax
And it's a fact that being black means you're under attack
And the worst enemies, your own kind
And at this rate of genocide
We don't have a long time
To repopulate he United States
No wonder Latinos have replaced us as the minority race
Awake or attend you own wake
Now's the time for us to educate
Ourselves so that we can be great
No longer grim statistics in society
No longer the majority of those in poverty
And I believe that we can be
Superior figures in every industry
Do you know it's in our genes to achieve
Do your own history
We descended from kings and queens
Have we forgotten what that really means
What it means is that we're royalty

And that it's in us to succeed
If we apply ourselves there's no boundary we can't exceed
Knowledge is the key
So that's what we need
Stop calling yourselves niggers because what you speak
Shows what you believe yourselves to be
Right now our future seems bleak
But we can change directions and head for victory

A wise man embraces change,
A fool stays the same

Chapter 5

A Mile in My Shoes

My Life

In my life
I've been through many wars
Acquired plenty scars
And some nights I'd just look up at the stars
Wondering if life was really meant to be so hard
Oh, my Lord
When You made me
Did You foresee?
The crazy
And troubled life that I would lead?
I've seen
The devil at his worst
And several times it could've been me riding in that hearse
My first mistake
Was when I rebelled at home
They say you don't miss the water...
Until the well is gone

Each life is a journey of ups and downs
Hills and valleys, however, the one who determines
Your destination......is YOU

Fallen Angel

If my soul ain't whole
Then who am I
And where am I going
I've been given a chance to fly
But somehow I'm not soaring
Not growing
And what a shame
'Cause in this game
I've been made a winner
Yet I live defeated as a sinner
My inner person
Despises the outer shell
For lust it's thirstin'
Traveling the highway to hell
A favorite child rebels
Favored by The Most High
Looked upon from the sky
With joy and pride
So I ask myself why
Why don't I fly
With the wings I've been given
Why oh why
Does a saint keep sinnin'

"A just man falls seven times…and rises up again…"
-Proverbs 24:16 (KJV Version)

Life Lessons

Caught in a vibe
Listening to Nas
Just glad to be alive
Even I'm surprised
Didn't think that I'd make it
Felt the shadow of death
And back then I couldn't shake it
Faced with two options I chose the cell
Instead of hell
The common tale for us young Black Males
Who continue to fail
You'd probably turn pale
If you could see through these eyes
What I've witnessed would make a dead man cry
Sometimes I
Wonder what's wrong with my mind
Why is it that I have these visions?
Though my body's inside my mind is free from prison
Some laugh at my condition
Think I'm just trippin'
Godly gifted, but no one listens
Guess it's just me and wisdom
That way there's no friction
My mission now is to make the best
Of every moment and breath
That's left inside of my chest
Gotta watch every step that I take
Cause to miscalculate
Could lead to mistakes
Many days
Reminisced on what my elders said
Probably never would've tread
These minefields had I heeded
The find gems that proceeded

From lips of experience
But when you're young and hip
None of it makes sense
Until you're in predicaments
You could've avoided
Wishing you could go back to all of the advice and record it
If I could reverse my past - I would
If I could reimburse my bads with good - I would
But that's not how it works
In life you fail first
Then learn from your hurts
But the good thing about that
Is you get to come back
From what you failed at
Armed with new insight
To make your sins right
After facing the darkest night
My future finally looks bright....
Thanks to the lessons I've learned in life.

How beautiful are the golden rays
Of light at the end of the tunnel

Made Me Stronger

My trails and tribulations
Made me stronger
What didn't kill me
Made me live longer
When I suffered hunger
My appetite to succeed increased
Stared into the eyes of the beast
And I'm still in one piece
I commanded disbelief to cease
And suppressed my fears
Because I only wish to unleash
Strength in my remaining years
And I'm still here
In spite of haters and animosity
Naysayers and backstabbing gossiping
What they thought would bring me down
Just inspired me
And I'm still around
After the conflicts and arguments
Trapped in a lifestyle of scandal and hard events
It's ironic, that what didn't break me
Only made me
What they thought would devastate me
Are the things that saved me
How amazing
It all made me stronger...
The pain, the shame,
Even the rain
Taught me to appreciate
When sunny days finally came
Transformed and changed
I gained force from the blows that assaulted me
Been a victim of wearers of uniforms and authorities
Spotlights pointed out all the flaws in me

Gunshots tried to make me deceased
Demons haunted my sleep
Yet I still found peace
Right in the eye of the storm
I found the greatest calm
Cause life goes on
Whether I cry or laugh
After the war's the aftermath
With some left alive
I fought my battles and I survived
Saw my soul collide into a wall of death
Felt hands press upon my neck
Trying to steal my last breath
Nevertheless, heavenly hands came to my rescue
There'll always be stress
Just don't let it get the best of you
It's only testing you
So stay cool
When the kitchen heats up
It's okay to get flustered
Just don't self-destruct
When volcanoes erupt in my life
I gather my strength and I fight
What didn't blind me gave me sight
From bright lights to dark nights
I had to stand my ground
In the ring with enemies around
But I refused to go down
In life either you swim or you drown
Cause ain't no life jackets to be found
In the ocean of city life
Where guns pop and bodies get sliced with knifes
And that's what it's really like
But it all made me stronger....
My tussles with deranged personalities
Strange characters that taunted and hassled me
Encountered ridiculous fools
Disrespectful dudes

In need of new attitudes
But I never came unglued
Because what didn't make me ignorant
Just took me to school
And in the end, it all made me stronger
Throughout my bouts with self-doubts
And mental torments
I chose to face it all rather than avoid it
From the hurt of unfaithful lovers
To the sharp repercussions of my very own blunders
What didn't make me old just made me younger
And it all made me stronger...
My journey to maturity and spiritual growth
My struggles and the accomplishment of my goals
The self discovery of my essence
My blessings and learned lessons
My family, mentors, and teachers
My mistakes and trial and error research
My studies and the sum of my learning
My successes and whole life's journey
My critics, as well as those who helped
My losses, gains, and even life itself
Rather than combine to form my demise
It all made me strong, more grown and wise.

"Adversity is the fertilizer in life's garden."

360

Trapped in a world of sin
But I somehow escaped
Now I find myself back in the same place
Enticed by the glamorous streets
I did everything to make ends meet
And most of the time
It was all the wrong things
The devil had me blind
And just a pawn in his game
Man was I lame
I never even saw it coming
Back then I was some green
But there's nothing
Like a nasty dose of reality
To snap you back from that fantasy
You've been comatose in
I had to learn that every grin ain't a friend
Learned that one the hard way
By getting played by smiling faces
Heartless bastards, but that's how they played it
It's a crazy jungle out here
So keep your eyes wide open
Don't let your enemies near
Put a cap on your fear
To survive you've got to be fierce
That's life 101
And that's a class you don't 'wanna flunk
'Cause if you fail it you're done
I tried to run
From the wages of my actions
But I guess I'm not a fast one
Because here I am captured
By my own devices
Cheap choices come with high prices

But that's just how life is
So it's best not to gripe, kid
Just suck it up like I did
I lay in the bed that I made
It was either that or the grave
When I was going through that young and foolish phase
I wouldn't behave
Out there acting stupid for days
Trying my best to get my face on the front page
But God wouldn't let it happen that way
By His grace
He brought me to a better place
Sat me down where I could concentrate
And change my ways
I was on a self-destructive rampage
But now I'm headed for better days

"If a tadpole can grow legs and jump high,
And a caterpillar can grow wings and fly,
Then surely I can make a change and transform my life."

Ain't Enough

I'm the batter
Life threw a curve ball
Everyday it's a battle
To be a man and stand tall
Seems like the more I give it my all
The more the drama erupts
The more I hope
Looks like it worsens my luck
But I will never give in or give up
No ifs, ands or buts
'Cause it just ain't enough
To hold me down
Turn me around
Or disassemble my crown
I give a care how it sounds
I'll bite, kick, or scratch not to hit the ground
Round for round
Blow after blow thrown at me
I'm in a zone full of fake laughter and slave master mentality
Here it is, a whole new millennium
And folks are walking around with the same hurtful sins in them
Looks like they're stuck
Fully corrupt
Chain-locked on self-destruct
But it still ain't enough
No matter how much
They put me through
I will not lose
I'm too focused to be confused
Mind sharp as a baboon's tooth
Not one screw is loose
So I'm alert when female serpents seduce
Enticing me to take a bite of the fruit
So I could fall like Adam
With no chance to regroup
My power lies in the truth
Calamity enters my life in groups

Jealously and envy surrounds me like army troops
And if they had their way, I'd be hung from a noose
But that's something they can never do
No matter what they put me through
I'll never give in or give up
No ifs, ands, or buts
My spirit refuses to be crushed
'Cause it just ain't enough
To hold me down,
Turn me around,
Or disassemble my crown
I was up even when they locked me down
And now 'gotta deal with stipulations and parole
And 'gotta walk a tight rope for these shiesty P.O.s
It's all a set back
Between sex and the set
It's all a death trap
And even more so when you've got a stripe on your back
And can't be strapped
It's like they're setting me up to get jacked
To get my head cracked
Is it opinion or fact?
Am I a man or a stat?
If it isn't this, then it's that
But it's always something
But I know one thing
True love can never be severed
I call fake friends fair weathers
'Cause when it rains they grow feathers
That's good though, because phonies flock together
It's unnatural for want-nothings to stand next to a go-getter
So really, their absence just makes me better
The next time I fall will be never
'Cause ain't none of it enough
To keep me from
Becoming the best I can become

Sometimes you reach the point
Where enough is enough

Ain't Going Back

Can't go back
I lack the vision for looking behind
Hustle and grind
It's time that I unleash and untie
My every talent inside
By utilizing my mind
Prioritize, strategize
Approach my goals
Step to the line
Live through my soul
Aggressively go after what's mine
Pace myself
Brace myself
To encounter opposition
Certain people make it their mission
For your demise they be constantly wishin'
Be gossiping and all in your business
But I just laugh
If only they knew the power I have
And while they're mad
I ascend like the smoke from a drag
On a cigarette
The greater the struggle
The bigger the prize the winner gets
And though I've stumbled
I'm now humbled
Yet stronger than ever
Made it out of the jungle
Had to tussle and rumble
But it made me better
Hardship made me a go-getter
And I will never
Go back to being anything lesser

You live and you learn

Explicit Refusal

I **refuse** to lose
I **refuse** to fail
I **refuse** to choose not to excel
I **refuse** to bail
Even when it feels like hell
I **refuse** to trail
I **refuse** to retreat
I **refuse** to dwell
In the land of defeat
I **refuse** to cease
The pursuit of my dreams
I **refuse** to follow
As oppose to lead
I **refuse** to not grow
To all that I'm supposed to be
Refuse to slow the speed
Of my forward progress
Refuse to let anything impede
On my need for success
I **refuse** to digress
Refuse to select backward steps
I **refuse** to reflect anything less
Than my absolute best
I **refuse** to be afraid
I **refuse** to fear
Refuse to let people's evil ways
Give me heartache and tears
I **refuse** to cower
When my enemies growl
I will use my power
So they can't pull me down'
I **refuse** to be pessimistic
When attacked with flak
And any virtuous characteristic
I **refuse** to lack

I **refuse** to crack
I **refuse** to crumble
I **refuse** to be held back
I **refuse** to stumble
I **refuse** to mumble
I **refuse** to complain
I **refuse** to grumble
Under my burdens and pain
I **refuse** to refrain from giving my all
I **refuse** to abstain from standing tall and strong
I **refuse** to fall
Even when my back's against the wall
I **refuse** to crawl
I **refuse** to bow
I **refuse** to let my problems
Push me around
I **refuse** to drown
In a sea of despair
I **refuse** to frown
Or pull out my hair
I choose to care
For my family and friends
It is soon I'll be there
If trouble ever begins
I **refuse** to break
When my burdens are great
I **refuse** to rattle or shake
Quake or disintegrate
I **refuse** to hate
Refuse to be phoney or fake
I **refuse** to slither like snakes
Con or manipulate
I **refuse** to participate
In things I don't believe in
The reason is
Life is a journey of choices
So I use my right to choose
What for me would be joyous...
But the rest I **refuse.**

THROUGH MY STRUGGLE

Through my struggle
I've learned to be a man
The road has been long and hard
But I finally understand
What it feels to be alive
And that true beauty can only be seen
Through a grateful pair of eyes

I had to go to the bottom
And struggle to rise
In order to appreciate
My blessings in life

Through my struggle
I found my true identity
At my weakest point
It was then that Heaven strengthened me
With a vision of my purpose
And my role in the grand scheme
It was in the midst of the struggle
That I discovered my dreams

Somewhere in the fire
And the peak of the storm
The relentless strength
Of your character is born

And through my struggle
I shed an ocean of tears
And was forced to conquer
My deepest fears

It got to the point
Where I had to believe in myself
And have the courage to move forward
In spite of everything else
It took everything I had
To make it through these struggles
But it taught me you can only reach greatness
By staying humble
And these are the lessons I learned
Through my struggles

Your journey reveals your purpose

Close My Eyes

Close my eyes
And visualize what I've become
The battle was hard
But thank the Lord that I've won
Can finally see the sun
After a million dark days
Where I laid
In a coffin in a self dug grave
Unable to find my way
Until I looked within
Locked the door of my demons
With the key of discipline
Just when it all seemed hopeless
Somewhere in the dark I saw a spark
And it brought me into focus
And I climbed out of the womb
Closed my eyes
And saw the outline of the moon
And then I realized
You can still win after you lose

Failure is the catapult to success

AMBITION

Learned my lesson
Now possessing
Keen perception
No more stressing
What a blessing

Now I'm testing
My new philosophy
Want to be
The author of my biography
Can't you see
Me
At the helm of my destiny
Navigating the seas
Hoping to reach eternity
On a journey shaded by
The clouds of hope in the sky
I've gotta try
Or life'll just keep passing me by
I won't lie
I'm hungry for a piece of the pie
No reason why I
Shouldn't satisfy
My desire to fly
With wings I could glide
Propelled by the winds of time
Non-stop
Straight to the top
Target the spot
And I've got to drop
Procrastination
From my mental equation
Won't let it take away from
My destination
Of upward ascension
Like a bird on a mission
My condition...
Is the state of ambition

Ambition is the fuel that burns my soul forward

Hidden Treasure

Meditation
Sharpens my concentration
Pulse pulsating with information
Got my nerves shaking
Like a mental patient
Who hasn't taken
His medication
Finally I've awakened
To realize
That I have something valuable inside
The gift of rhyme
Sun shined on my mind
The day that I tried
The day I arrived
No way could I lie
Or try to hide
The beautiful butterfly
That lay deep inside
So I opened my soul wide
Took to the sky
And spread my wings and let it fly

"There's a beautiful butterfly inside of us all."

Just a Man

Being a man is something that's hard to define
We go through things that are hard to explain at times
And our minds just feel pressed from all sides
Even when we smile
There's a pain deep inside
I often cry
Cause the hurt I feel is so real
There's an empty space in my life
That needs to be filled
And until all of my wounds heal
I'll still continue to pray
And have faith that God will make a way
Out of this maze which I cannot escape
Please understand
That I am only a man
And I try my best
But sometimes I fail the test
It's like I need emotional rest
Because the things I go through be having me stressed
Draining me of all I have left
I need a vest
It's like the world's shooting bullets at my chest
I wasn't born with a silver spoon in my hand
My whole life span
No one gave a damn
I have to make it the best way that I can
But that's okay cause I'm a man
Therefore I am what I am
And I just need you to understand
That I'm just a man

Even Superman gets weary at times

None of this makes sense
But then again
Maybe this is the way it was meant
So many riddles it'll
Make your head spin
Which way is the end
And when can I begin to descend
This whirl wind
I'm swirlin' in

At times life seems like an endless maze
with no points of direction

My Sole Aspiration

Spending my prime
Doing jail time
Never thought as a kid
That I'd be doing a bid
But that's how it is
In this world we live
One wrong turn
Could get you burned
Beyond recognition
People tried to show me the right way but still I wouldn't listen
Now this is what I'm getting
And really it's all on me
For willingly
Surrendering my dignity
But does that mean
I should no longer be seen
As a human being
Everyone's done something wrong in their lives
But it's mostly my kind that gets ostracized
Am I wrong or right
But I won't gripe
Cause that won't change what's already been arranged
The best I can do is maintain
And go on from here
Prioritize my life and make my goals clear
But my biggest fear
Is that I won't arrive
At the place I aspire
Which is to be a citizen of God's empire
Because that destination....
Is my sole aspiration

Failure is not a life sentence
As long as there is life in your body
You can make a change for the better

Non-Compliant

I'm an antagonist
Of the establishment
Instead of flow I'd rather go against
Contemporary conformities
If that makes me stand out, so let it be
Too many Indians but not me
I'm the chief of my destiny
Following only where I lead
And radically I stand apart
Embracing my ideology
Like light in the dark
With all my heart I renounce the ways of modern society
Not even phased by the ways that it lies to me
I'm not deceived
Clearly my eyes see through the matrix
To the reality of what makes it
The way it is
In the place we live
So glib and oppressive
Everyone traveling paths that are corrosive
Stumbling to contribute to the explosive
Climate of global degradation
Bringing the orb closer to its own elimination
Think I'm gonna' conform to the norm or the status quo
My answer to that...is hell no!

Stand for something
Or fall for anything

On My Own

I'm trying to get myself together
Been through the stormiest weather
Which seemed to last forever
And get wetter and wetter
Guess I'm better at being a man
After being broken to the bone
A young soul out in the world
All soaked and alone
Searching for a place to call home
On my own
Like a lone wolf in the middle of nowhere
Surrounded by lions, tigers, and bears
But I ain't scared
Just on my own
And I'm grown, so I can't complain
But the fact remains
And that doesn't slacken the pain
I played the game
And it played me back
Sped through life like a train
Then jumped right off track
Young and black
And I wonder if that's
Got anything to do with the stripe on my back
Been under attack since birth
Fighting them and us
Don't know which hurts
What am I worth?
I'm treated like the scum of the Earth
Lower than dirt
Tried it all but none of it worked
I'm on my own
But still going strong
All day and all night long
Won't stop till the last breath's gone
And that fat lady starts singing her favorite song
I'll be standing alone
Proud and strong
Still holding my own

"As long as God is on the thrown...you are never alone."

Revolutionary

Audibly
Verbally
Literarilly
Anyway I can, I'm a revolutionary
And visionary for my people
And I won't sleep good
Until it's understood by all
That we're going to stand tall
And not crawl
I represent us
Until there's no breath left
To me it's a must
And I'm committed till death
Even if I have to sacrifice my life
I'm gonna' champion my people's cause
And never pause because I know that it's right
The shadow of night
Envelopes our landscape
But I know that there's a way
To translate our gloom into a brighter day
As a revolutionary it's primary
That I revolutionize
There's no disguise
I'm fighting for my people's lives
Tired of seeing tears falling from their eyes
Tired of hearing the cries
Y'all it's time to rise
Fallen kings and queens
Spread your wings
Into the heavens spring quick
From the ashes everlasting like the phoenix
And my dream is
That one day we'll love each other
And become formidable men and women of color
In mansions and out the gutter
CEO's that control and employ
Builders of communities instead of those who destroy
Creative engineers that design

Instead of ex-cons serving time
Behind bars
Since a little boy
I've wished we would connect
As one and show each other respect
Laboring together to achieve what is best
With resurrection as our number one quest
Before we pass from this life to the next
I must express positively
That with fierceness, love and loyalty
I will always be
Your revolutionary

The voice of truth rings loud
To those who are willing to hear

UNSTOPPABLE

How can you stop me
How can you end this
Giving up is not me
I'm too relentless
The day I finish
Is the day they lower me
Into the Earth
And cover dirt over me
And even then still I'll be around
My words, my poetry
Will give my spirit sound
How can you suppress me
My actions can attest
To the fact that there's no arresting me
I'm addressing the powers that be
That constantly seek
Ways to keep
Me under their feet
But their actions are fruitless
Irrelevant and totally useless
'Cause I refuse to meet defeat
Run or retreat
Pout or cry myself to sleep
You can not stop me
You can not lock me
My mind, my philosophy
Keep me constantly, unstoppably free
Therefore to stop me is impossible
Because I am..unstoppable

There is nothing in the world
That can stand in the way
Of someone who is determined

Chapter 6

When Love Hurts

When Love Hurts

Introduced me to
A pain I never knew
So strongly swept by you
Your charm dimmed my view
Hooked me like a saber's tooth
I guess it's true
That love hurts
Makes me wish my heart would not work
I feel like such a jerk
To allow myself to fall
Be captured and enthralled
How could love make a strong man crawl
Where is my pride
Where is my dignity
I need them to arrive
And relinquish me
From this merciless captor
Lord knows
I need to close the book on this chapter

Love can either be the highest high
Or the lowest low

I Should've Known

If only I knew then
The things I now know and understand
If only I knew as a boy
What it took to be a man
Maybe I should've been wise
At the time when I was ignorant
But how does one with now schooling
Prove himself intelligent
If I did know these things then
I would've been spared a lot of pain
And sorrow that develops
Into an ocean of tears that fall like rain
If only I knew that life
Should be spent sharing and loving
Instead of the chaos
In this world of pushing and shoving
I should've known then that love should be sincere
Instead of falsely spoken
And why did it take so long for me to realize
That hearts should be nurtured and not broken
If only I could've know that God is kind
And graceful in every way
That He is the One that gives us strength
And opens our eyes to every waking day
One thing's for sure
Life's lessons aren't learned overnight
But through a step by step process
I didn't know those things then, but I do now
So what's next

Hindsight is the clearest vision

INADEQUATE

You're the one I wanted to chain myself with
But I've learned that you're inadequate
And we don't fit
My ideas of a relationship
You're too stiff
And now that I've gotten a grip
On this situation
I think its time to walk away from
This pent up frustration
That make us
Deflate trust
We constantly fuss
So what's being accomplished
When all that we promised
Has vanished to yesterday
Today our lips don't even know what to say
All I want is to go my separate way
Because a new life awaits
And someone who'll appreciate
The treasure you considered waste
But it's over and I'm glad of it
Because I've finally realize...
That you're inadequate

One person's trash
Is another's treasure

NEVER AGAIN

I should've known not to hope
Should've known that what appeared would vanish like smoke
How could I be so foolish from the start?
How could I so freely give away my delicate heart?
Always falling so easily
Often finding myself crying in my sleep
So many promises when it begins
Affectionate words and vows to always be friends
How wonderful it seems then
So many plans, so many dreams
And then it gets ugly and mean
Fussing and arguing
Attitudes about the little things
To your friends you're listening
As they offer tips
For your relationship
Whatever they said made you call it quits
Now you're back where you started from
You, the little ones, and no other one
But you had a good thing and didn't realize
That this type of thing happens once in a lifetime
Threw it away over one disagreement
Despite receiving a royal treatment
It's like being blessed with a treasure box
Then throwing it away because of one rock
But all the rest of its contents are wonderful
Sparkly and shiny like gold
Yet you've cast it all aside and only God knows
Where it goes now
But I'll never do this again...
No way, no how

Regret leaves a wound that lingers

Could It Be?

Could it be
There's something wrong with me
Why do people see
What they consider to be abnormality
Where do they get the audacity
It's their own inadequacy
That's got them mad at me
The bound all ways envy the free
Just as the shore longingly
Wants to become a part of the sea
Could it be
A form of jealousy
When all I hear is mockery
Can't help that I do things properly
I was genetically engineered to achieve
So naturally it's my ability
To supersede the lowly
It's done involuntarily
My personality exudes charisma
So what is the problem with that
Guess my strengths magnify what others lack
So they attack
And their form of combat is to label me as weird
But their eyes reveal that I'm just feared...
And that's the real deal

If you stopped to think about what others thought of you
You'd never get anywhere in life

Cold Turkey

Even though
You had me gone back then
I want you to know
I'll never travel that road again
I'll never run behind you
Like the fool I once was
I chased after you
Like a junky on drugs
And there I was
Strung out
With the shakes and shivers
Fiending for something
That only you could deliver
And every now and then
You'd give me a taste
Of that which
I so desperately craved
Which was only you
And then you'd snatch it away
From my touch and my view
Leaving me so confused
Not knowing what to do
And even though
I'm not bitter or angry
I have rid myself
Of the addiction that shamed me

Some habits if not kicked
will kick you

Concrete Heart

My heart is hard
Busted, bruised, and scarred
Battle-weary from so many wars
Fought on the front lines of my everyday life
So much strife
They pierce me like
Daggers that slice
Away my happy days
Just to hold a smile on my face
What a price I have to pay
They made my heart callous this way
Like sand-paper they scratched me with hate
And it affected me deeply
To the ground they beat me
What made them treat me so beastly
How could I not but fortify my heart
From the razor sharp darts
That made me their mark
They broke my smiles apart
And cut my laughter short
Like sharks they tried to eat me alive
But I refuse to die
Because I choose to survive
That's why my
Heart is armor plated
Stronger I've made it
To take the blows that I've traded
With the world
And all the turmoil that I'm faced with
Ate too many hardship pies
Drank too many soda pop lies
Got slapped in the face one too many times
Now I'm unblind
Unstupified
Unwilling to be kicked in the behind
Dried my eyes a long time ago
No more tears
Though for years they ran slow
I shut the valve off
The heart once soft
Is now hard like African diamonds
Guarded by retarded lions
With granite walls so tall that no one can climb in
My heart is concrete
Thanks to you society
If I smiled you growled at me
If I cried you mocked at me
Made sure that I was not happy
And all that was good..it by-passed me
So logically my heart turned hard
Protected by gates that are electrically charged
With burglar bars and alarms
To guard against intruders
'Cause I refuse to be hurt again
And I refuse to be drug in the dirt by you jerks again

A scorned heart never forgets

Relief

When the virus has gone
And the pain subsided
And all that was wrong
Is no longer private
Then comes relief
Comfort and peace
Used to be
I'd toss in my sleep
Now I just yawn and count sheep
Envisioning my dreams and fantasies
It was a she
Who cut me deep
Attacked me
With emotional teeth
But after pain came recovery
Now I'm at ease
And so relieved

It is so refreshing to come out of a bad situation
Like being born again

Chapter 7

In the Belly of the Beast

Swirlin'

It gets no realer
Than this thriller taking place
On my daily base
Too many demons to face
And the weights of the burdens are great
That inhabit my space
Am I asleep or awake
It's hard to concentrate
I hate the taste of the cake
That fate has baked
And placed on my plate
I pray for the magical words to say
To make it all go away
Like Dorothy and Toto I don't want to stay
In the land that's become an Oz to me
I'm tired of being
A participant in this odyssey
But I do see
What deceit won't let the blind visualize
Coded realities that hide
All that's wise from the eyes
Of the uncivilized
Too many try
To educate
But fools hate
Knowledge, because to them it's a waste
What monsters the system creates
It breaks
The will of those souls that chose not to know
And therefore couldn't grow
Or go
Beyond the foggy mist of ignorance
To the clear events of consciousness

Dysfunctional Residence

My home is a box

My songs are the ticks and the tocks

That play on the clocks

Nonstop

My home is the home of many

Where there's no sympathy

Just a symphony

Of voices ringing constantly

Eyes watching me like zombies

With high beams in the night

Projection of blind dreams

Shot down in flight

White hot darts shot by the enemy on side

Everywhere I turn

I learn there's a serpent nearby

Why cry

My life at home Is like a blizzard

In mid-December

Colder than arctic winters

Only the foulest sinners get this punishment

Dear God, whatever I did, I repent

Make it end

Give me a new home where it's not like this

One person's nightmare
Is another's reality

BIRD SONG

Like a bird
In caged habitation
My soul can be heard
Singing of liberation
As frustration takes away from patience
I crave the wave
Of wind beneath my wings
And oh how I thirst
For a taste of sweet mountainous streams
I dream of Spring
And lovely weather
And sun rays that Illuminate
The beauty of my feathers
Cause being free
Is better than captivation
Its hard to breathe
Apart from liberation
So liberate me
That I may be complete
And lay this beast
Of misery to sleep
That I may fly again
Embrace the sky again
Never to cry again
Cause to die in the wind...
Would be better than living while caged in

"Some birds aren't meant to be caged in,
Their feathers are just too bright"
---Morgan Freeman, "The Shawshank Redemption"

INFECTED

It's like I'm a contagious plague
The world acts like I'm dead
In every way I'm outcast
From a society segmented by class
Placed at the bottom of a barrel filled with trash
Acceptance removed from within my grasp
And everyone laughs
Because what I call a life
Is a nightmare in everyone else's sight
My hopes become dark as night
As each moment presents a new foe to fight
And like a knight
I try valiantly
To break free
From the stereotypes that assassinate me
But it's like a disease surrounding my essence
And it seems
Folk would rather die than be in my presence
Fearing contraction of the terrible plague I contain
Not wanting to be associated with the shame that it brings
Therefore I must change my state of affairs
And rid myself of this plague that I bear
I've got to find a vaccine
Something that'll make me clean
And be my remedy
From this plague that I bear

What would happen if God judged us
The way we judge others?

Nightmare

Imagine being alone for seven years
Shedding tears on the inside
Viewing life from a dim side
No one there to love or care
Gotta toughen up to bear the load
Or be the victim of this episode
Unload but never fold
Stay on guard till the end
Wanting to be normal but can't reveal what's within
From beginning to end, situation to situation
Everything I see fills me with frustration
I need a vacation from this place
Somewhere I could show my real face
Maybe even go on a date
At this rate I'm losing my tolerance for being alone
I'd like to spend time with someone instead of calling on the phone
When no one's home
It all went wrong
For in the midst of the calm
I penned my saddest song
So long I've mourned
Suffering from a heart that's torn
No one wants to open their arms and give you a hug
Guess when you're a number you're not entitled to love
What was I thinking of
Believing the promises that friends made
Empty words and feelings just fade
More and more everyday
Betrayed by those held so dear
Watched in tears as they all disappeared
Making everything I feared come true..
What a nightmare I've awakened to

The hardest bed to lay in...
Is the one you've made for yourself

A Prisoner's Dream

If I could be there I'd be the happiest of all men
I'd catch up on so many things, see so many places
Don't know where to begin

If I could be there the grass would be greener
The air fresher and sweet
Oh if I could just be there for a little while
It would be tastier than the tastiest treat

If I could just be there I'd be a better man
Like the Army I'd be all that I could be and go so far
I'd fly like a bird with beautiful wings
And marvel at how beautiful the clouds are

If I could be there I'd kiss my mom
And hug everyone I've ever cared about
I'd climb the highest building and thank the Lord
Boy would I shout!

I'd say my blessings at every meal
Cherish every sight that flashed before my eyes
To life I'd say hello...
No time for good byes

No more dirty showers with people all around
No more of the nasty food I ate
I'd be lounging on a beach in the Caribbean relaxing
While a gorgeous young lady feeds me grapes
Boy if I could only be there

*"You don't miss your water,
Until your well runs dry"*
--Unknown

X-RAY VISION

I see beyond the fences
Past the trenches
Of this war of which I'm a prisoner

Caught in the web of the law
Trying to undo the effects of this blunder
The one that almost took me under

It's a wonder
That when the blasts from the psychological weaponry
Produced so many casualties
And when the toes were tagged with identities
Surprisingly
None of them were me

Now I'm filled with glee
And optimism
And I see
Beyond the prism
Of the battle field with an eagle's vision

Beyond the prison bars
Stronger from all of the wounds and scars
Acquired during this excursion
Of obstacles, land mines, and diversions

Now I'm ready to stand
Equipped for the task at hand
Which is to be a man
Who isn't programmed
To be a kamakazi
Or some crash test dummy
For a cause that has nothing to do with me

Thank God I see
Beyond the razor fences
Past the contradictions
Of "good time"
That play games with my mind
Broadcasting lies, false alibis and foolish convos
Of past episodes
Bragging on the way we've thrown
Our lives away for this concrete trap
It's funny, but not to be laughed at

And yet I see
Beyond the fantasies
And all the letters from people writing me
Selling me dreams
To what is actually reality
That there's a better place ahead for me
And life after D.O.C.

The sharp lash of repercussions
Can convince the most stubborn person to change

Through the Storm

I made it through the storm
The lightening and the thunder
The world tried to take me under
The undertaker came
To lock me in chains
They amputated my brain
And changed my name
Into a number
Ten Winters and ten Summers
Ain't getting no younger
As the best years of my life
Slid down the drainage pipe
It just ain't right
But I kept my lips shut tight
What use is it to gripe
Might as well just fight
And persevere in spite
Of all that has mounted against me
Set my fears aside
And commenced to pounding relentlessly
Though endlessly the storm rages
I had to unleash the braveness
From within my inner cages
Many days it seemed
My life was just a bad dream
No one on my team
I had to go it alone
I looked for my friends but they were gone
So I braved the thunder storms on my own
They said I wouldn't
But I had to make it
They thought I couldn't
But I am fully persuaded
That I can hurdle my set backs

And the blemishes that stain my record black
"Kaboom" was the sound of the lightening crack
That almost struck me down
I ran but fell to the ground
And almost drowned
As black clouds poured acid rain from the sky
Sometimes I cried
But overall, the pain accelerated my drive
Here is a statement that I can say with pride...
I faced my storms...
And I survived

Struggles and challenges are the parents of success

RESURRECTION

As I awake from my slumber
Held under
In society's grave
Inmate ain't nothing but a modern way
Of saying slave
Anyway I'm now awake
Took ten years to shake death's embrace
Though now I elevate after seeing the reaper's face
But it was close
Several times I almost lost hope
But the more I struggle the more I grow
And so I soon arrive at the pearly gates
A smooth escape from jail house hate
And guards that make
The cells one hell of a place
A whole decade...what a waste
What a way to flourish my manhood
Would've ran if I could
But like a man I stood
Looked the judge in his eye when he hit that wood
And took my lick
And I won't lie, a few times I cried
But that was it
What sense is it to mourn
Sucked it up and moved on
Put on my rain jacket
And I challenged the storm
From dusk till dawn
Had to keep my armor on
Never knew when
The battle would erupt again
I had to make it clear
That I won't bend and I won't fear
Anyway I'm now awake
Did what it takes to make the cycle break
It'll never be me
Who proceeds through revolving doors
Snatched me from the streets and my peeps
But never no more
Ask how I know
And I'll show you how they break down champs
Reducing kings to play things
In these concentration camps

And no one gives a damn
Not even your 'fam
When you're on the other side
Feels like you've died
And might as well
'Cause it's hot as hell
In these cells we dwell
I hate the tastes
I hate the smells
Hate not receiving mail or visits
Hate sitting here reminiscing
Constantly missing
All I left behind
Stuck here on the front lines
Listening to lies told by cons with serpentine eyes
Asked myself why
Why volunteer to die
Why commit suicide
Is this what I deserve
It's so different from what I heard
That it's cool to act a fool and smoke herb
Jump in a ride and swerve
But no one said a word
About the repercussions
Or sleep interruptions
By goon squad looking Russians
Rushing at you full force
Swinging clubs with no remorse
And it ain't no joke
When your appeal gets denied in court
It kills your soul
In ways you'd never know
And so I arose
In those extreme conditions
Retrieved my wings and flew past the tension
Beyond the bricks,
The conflicts, and the friction
This is my ascension
This is my rise
I am now alive....
With eyes open wide

In the womb of despair miracles are born

Chapter 8

It Takes a Village

True Love

(To Momma)

You've given me true love
With an unconditional smile
You're my angel from above
Who's been there from my birth until now
It amazes me how
Wonderful the glow of your heart
Has illuminated my world like the stars
Though times have been hard
Your love remained the same from the start
On the canvas of my heart
You've painted the most beautiful art
Truly you are
My heart's pride and joy
When I was empty you filled my voids
All of my fears you destroyed
Darned right I'm a Mama's boy
And I love you like there's no tomorrow
If I needed, you went and borrowed
Even if it caused you sorrow
You're a miracle in a human torso
Whose love is true and pure
Unconditional and sure
Not once have you left us
No matter what, you never gave up
And from our lives you never budged
But all ways gave your precious love

"As endless as the universe,
So is a mother's love."

Definition of a Family

There was never given a greater gift to me
Than the family God has given me so gracefully

A family is the ones you should love
And the ones who'll always be there
They're the ones that you can lean on
When life's burdens are too much to bear

A family is the people
Who love you whether you're young or old
They're the people who'll kiss you on your cheek
And warm you when it's cold

A good family is something that everyone should wish for
Because when you're down and things seem dark
Your family's love will shine brighter than a star

The Bible tells me to love my father
And cherish my mother
Love your parents with all of your heart
Because they love you more than any other

A family is the foundation
On which sits the pillars of life

Birth of a Friendship

I'm glad that we met
I hope that we keep in touch
Because everyone needs a friend
For comfort when it's rough
I like how we met
Through the friend of a friend
And a friendship is precious
Something that should never end
I don't know if it was fate
Or maybe it was destiny
That decided to send me a comforter
For the times when I am lonely
Whatever it was
I know that I will never forget
The wonderful gift that was given to me
On the day that we met

"There is a friend that sticks
Closer than a brother."
(Proverbs 18:24)

I Appreciate You

I appreciate you
And the things you say and do
That make me feel so good
I swear, knock on wood
The joy you've brought into my life
Shines like a ray of light
Into the dark and lonely parts
Of my soul, mind and heart
I wish that I could hold your hand
And make you understand
That you are touching me inside
So gently I can't hide
From your sweetness
That's like a gentle touch
I'm so grateful to have met you
And I appreciate you so much

"Good deeds are seeds planted in the garden of someone's life;
The fruit of which will bless the planter."

Maternal Devotion

My dear mother
To me there's no one above her
Except the Lord of course
So this poem I wrote
Just to let you know
That my love will always be yours
Forever and ever
Even in heaven
We'll always be together
'Cause our bond could never be severed
But only get better and better
Even when there's stormy weather
We make it through
Because our strength comes from you know Who
He made you a tree
And I'm your fruit
So I will always be
Lovingly
Devoted to you

FRIENDSHIP

Friendship is the beginning
Of something special from above
It's the road that leads
To the neighborhood of love
When times get hard
It's good to have
A friend by your side
To comfort and support you
And wipe the tears from your eyes
A friend will make you laugh
When you're ready to cry
And he'll stand by your side
Whether you're wrong or right
Throughout life a friend will be there
To take care of you
He'll put a smile on your face
And always tell you the truth
And love you for you
A friend is someone with whom
You could clown and act crazy around
They're there to lift your spirits
When you're feeling down
It might sound wild
But a friend is worth more than diamonds and gold
A friend will warm you when it's cold
And love you
From the deepest part of their soul
Whether you're young or old
Rich, poor, single, or married
It's a blessing to have a friend
Because friendship is everlasting

When you're feeling foul
A friend can make you smile

So So Special

Can't wait to be with you again
I hope that soon is when
We'll attend our reunion
So long I've missed you my friend
Mother and sister in Christ
Gave me life
Then sacrificed your life to raise me right
Even though I went the wrong direction
Believe me I've learned my lesson
And even though I'm not the greatest son yet
Before you go I'll make sure I'm a success
'Cause you're the best
And I'm gonna' make you proud
Make you smile
'Cause you're the love of my life and the cloud
That gives shade to my heart when I'm down and out
Even when I pout
Always patient with me
That's why I can't wait to see
Your face when I'm finally free
I just want you to see
That you mean the world to me

Mother

The word mother defined
Is the person who gives birth to you
But she's so much more
She's the one who's there in your time of need
And the one you should adore
I have a mother
Who'd warm me when I'm cold
She takes good care of her family
And has a heart of pure gold
It seems to me
That I am my mother's pride and joy
And she mine
Her love and protection
Beams on me like the brightest day's sunshine
Personally I think my mom should be given
The greatest mom award
For her duties are well done
And I am more than proud
To be called her son
I can go on and on about my mother
I know my siblings feel the same
For she's the greatest mom of all
And should be inducted into the mom's hall of fame

Words of a Friend

If I could
I'd be there for you
As someone who'd
Help you through
Your trials and struggles
Offer my hand when you stumble
Lay down my coat in a puddle
And welcome you into open arms
When you need to be warmed
From the cold world
Lonely girl
You're a precious pearl
So never give up on you
For nothing's great enough to
Annihilate your spirit
Now's the time, I feel it
Nicer things are coming your way
Everyday your strength takes shape
And you're getting better
At handling life, and learning to weather
The storms
For you are strong
Tough times don't last long
They do move on
They're only here to test us
Eventually you'll reach success, but
Never forget where you've come from
Precious one
Your future is as bright as the sun
So have fun
While you're young
For your life has just begun

"As iron sharpens iron,
So does a man sharpen the countenance of his friend"
-Proverbs 27:17

YOUR SEED

(To Daddy)

Behold the seed you sowed
In a perilous world it grows
Despite its foes
And destructive elements
Sent to cause its end
It wouldn't relent
In spite of famine
And lack of rain from the sky
It continued to thrive
Determined to survive
It refused to die
And no one knew why
The roots grew and thickened
As it blossomed with fruit in the worst conditions
Throughout the heat and rainy seasons
Its tenacity defied conventional reason
Though it faced some storms and confronted some winds
And in the process it lost a few limbs
Yet it possessed a strength from within
It just wouldn't give in
This little seed
You planted so long ago
Conquered the weeds
That tried to inhibit its growth
I know that at one time
Seemed like it wouldn't make it
But no matter how hard they tried
They just couldn't break it
I am the seed once small
Now standing tall
Through Winter, Spring, and Fall
Remaining calm throughout life's storms
As I persevere
Growing stronger and stronger every year
This is the history of the sapling
That became the greatest tree
And that tree is me...
Your seed

The more I struggle, the more I grow

Afterthought

After reading this book, it is my sincere and humble prayer that something positive was gained by you, the reader. I am honored that you chose to listen to what I had to say. And I hope that you have been touched in some way positively by something contained within these pages. Please know that I wrote from the heart from what I've seen and experienced in my life. May you all be blessed by our Most High God. And may there be no excuses for you making your dreams come true.

About the Author

James Hudson, Jr. Is a God fearing poet and motivational speaker. Born and raised in New Orleans, Louisiana he was in an automobile accident at the tender age of 5 that broke every bone in his body and left him in a body cast for months. He had to learn how to walk again. And thus began his journey of a mindset that you can overcome anything life throws your way...if only you believe and have the will to press on. He travels the world motivating others to be their greatest selves with No Excuses!

www.ingramcontent.com/pod-product-compliance
Lightning Source LLC
LaVergne TN
LVHW010056110826
845155LV00028B/371

* 9 7 8 1 9 3 4 0 6 0 6 1 2 *